CHART SHAPES

THE CODE TO INTERPRETATION

Wanda Sellar

The Wessex Astrologer

Published in English in 2019 by
The Wessex Astrologer Ltd
PO Box 9307
Swanage
BH19 9BF

For a full list of our titles go to www.wessexastrologer.com

Cover design by Jonathan Taylor

A catalogue record for this book is available at The British Library

ISBN 9781910531389

Contents

1

Chart Patterns and the Code to Interpretation

Chart Patterns

Chart shapes or patterns refers to a relatively modern concept, pioneered by Marc Edmund Jones* and further developed by Robert C. Jansky.**

Apart from suggesting the basis of character, the chart shape or pattern can answer the oft, albeit silent, question: where do I begin? Therefore the chart shape can initiate the departure point for chart interpretation, acting as a springboard towards a structured, step-by-step procedure for analysis.

A quick glance cannot always decide the actual shape of the chart. It can take a while to adjust the eye to the shape before a decision is made. If at times a chart looks as if it might belong to two shapes, there are designated degrees for separating groups of planets.

Astrologers may even differ in what they see. Maybe it can be likened to a Rorschach test, a psychological perception test, where the individual decides what the shape may be. Likewise, the final judgement of shape should rest with the delineating astrologer. The aim after all is not to make the chart fit into a shape, like the proverbial shoe, but act as a spur to interpretation.

No chart shape, however, whether amongst the seven designated shapes, or a mixture of them, is better or worse than any other. Human beings are complex, and the more complex they are, so will their charts be.

Not all charts fall into the idealised chart patterns, or even their designated variations, and both Jones and Jansky admit this. However, this is not a problem, and in fact can be an aid to interpretation. In such a case, one should examine the planet/s which deviate from the designated shape. They often turn out to be the High Focus Planet which leads the interpretation. This is further explained in Chapter 9, Mixed and Irregular Shapes, with chart examples.

Or indeed, a chart refuses to fall into one shape or another and seems to be a mixture of two. Jansky is adamant that one shape has to be chosen over the other if there is a choice. Maybe one should consider one to be the dominating shape, but influenced by another. Rather than creating a problem; it could be even more exciting in terms of interpretation.

The rules of judgment

To judge the type of shape, only the ten planets should be taken into consideration; this excludes the Ascendant, Midheaven, the Nodes, Chiron and any other points the astrologer utilises in his or her usual analysis. All these points can ultimately be included in interpretation of course, but initial judgement of shape should be made on the ten planets alone: seven traditional planets and three modern planets.

In each chart shape, certain rules are laid down as to designated number of degrees between groups of planets, but this should act more as a guide rather than an unalterable dictum. Perhaps more importance can be given to how the shape appears visually than counting the actual degrees.

Judgement

In many chart shapes, a planet stands out as the focal planet, which Jones and Jansky refer to as the High Focus planet. Judging the strength of this planet is by usual methods using the traditional dignities and debilities; differentiating between the angular, succedent and cadent houses, as well as aspects to other planets. A planet that is retrograde or stationary is likely to also impact on interpretation. (See Appendix).

If the High Focus planet is judged to be strong, then things happen easily or circumstances in life facilitate an easier route to success. If the High Focus planet is judged to be weak, then more effort is needed to achieve aims. The challenge is not to give in at the first difficult or seemingly insurmountable hurdle.

If the High Focus planet is a benefic – Venus or Jupiter – or is aspected by one of the benefics, then there is a certain amount of luck or good fortune attending the individual's aims in life. He or she may be born into a wealthy family or have influential friends to smooth the path to success. If the High Focus planet is a malefic – Mars and Saturn – or in aspect to one of the malefics, then success is not necessarily denied, but there are greater challenges to overcome. Usually in such cases, the individual has to rely upon his or her own resources for achievement.

A High Focus planet in aspect to the nodes may suggest a connection to the public, often bestowing popularity.

Boundary planets

In many shapes there are isolating planets highlighting certain areas in life. These are referred to as boundary planets, with one leading planet, sometimes called the cutting planet by different astrologers, and a trailing planet.

To find the boundary planets start in the empty part of the chart – signs and houses – and move anti-clockwise towards the first planet in order of signs. The first planet encountered is the leading planet, and the last planet following the rest through the signs is the trailing planet.

It is thought that there may well be a more passive energy in the trailing planet compared to the leading planet. Its strength should also be judged. If strong, then plans and goals tend to end well, speaking in general terms. Endeavours reach a successful conclusion. Though this can sometimes be seen as a kind of support to the leading planet that is not at first obvious.

If the trailing planet is weak, then there is a possibility that things do not end well, perhaps because there either hasn't been enough attention given to life procedures, or there might be a tendency not to see things through for some reason, or lack of confidence and belief. The astrologer may be able to point this out in consultation; awareness of weaknesses or difficulties may encourage willpower to deal with such matters.

Another focus in the chart involves the midpoints which are principally linked to the boundary planets, but this will be further explained with explanation of chart shapes and the chart delineation that follows.

Associated Planets

Each chart shape appears to be associated with a particular planet: this doesn't appear to be something M.E. Jones proposed but through various writings on this subject, principally with R. Jansky, it seems that astrologers associate a chart shape with a planet or sign. For instance Mercury with the Splash chart, Mars with the Locomotive shape, and Venus with the See-Saw chart. See below for a conjectured view of planetary associations and the underlying reasons for choice.

Chart Shape	Associated Planet
Splash	Mercury
Locomotive	Mars
Bowl	The Moon

Bucket
    Sling Variety
    Two Handle Variety
    Conjunction Variety
	Jupiter

See-Saw
    Hourglass
    Butterfly
	Venus

Splay Tripod	The Sun
Bundle Fanhandle	Saturn

The Splash chart which tends to give diversity of interests and a life of variety accords best with Mercury the planet of mental acuity and virtuosity.

The Locomotive chart with its rush towards a goal links very well with the planet Mars, known for speedy action and assertion.

The Bowl chart, which tends to act as a container to activities and goals, has almost the shape of the Moon, and indeed this planet acts to contain, secure and safeguard its possessions and feelings.

The Bucket/Basket chart, which has a solitary planet leading the way is like the thunderbolt of Jupiter, often following a designated trajectory. (This includes the variation: Sling, Conjunction, Two Handles).

The See-Saw chart tries to achieve harmony, so the obvious planetary association is Venus which endeavours to foster a balance in all spheres of activity. (This includes the variation, Hourglass).

The Splay shape, with its penchant for individualism, tries to make some sort of original statement which might accord well with the Sun with its drive towards (w)holism through gathering disparate ideas. (This includes the Tripod variation.)

The Wedge/Bundle shape looking neither right nor left but moving steadily towards a goal on its own terms, has Saturn in its wake, since this planet adheres to stability and rigidity.

Generally speaking the Bucket and See-Saw shapes, both associated with the benefics Venus and Jupiter, suggest a life that is helped along by luck, frequent opportunities and with aid from others. The tendency may be however, to rely too much on luck and not safeguard one's investment in projects.

The Locomotive and Bundle, linked to the malefics, Mars and Saturn, challenge the individual to rely more on his own devices and create his own opportunities for advancement. Opportunities may not be easily forthcoming but greater care given to investment in projects could reap dividends.

The Bowl chart, associated with the Moon may draw the individual towards the public domain. The Splash, and its associated planet Mercury, gives a predilection towards opportunity through risk as it gathers experiences of a diverse nature.

General Analysis

Planetary handles, singletons and boundary planets should be judged by type of signs within the triplicities and quadruplicities, as well as houses, such as angular, succedent or cadent.

Although the shape of the chart is customarily judged by just the ten planets, there are occasions when another point in the chart, such as the nodes, Chiron, the dark Moon Lilith, Part of Fortune, or any other point favoured by the astrologer, may stand out. For instance a Bowl chart which contains all the ten planets may have one of the aforementioned points in the opposite hemisphere acting as a handle. Whilst the chart still remains a Bowl, the singleton opposite, whatever it may be, should play an important part in the analysis.

Or a designated Locomotive chart may have Chiron positioned just before the leading or trailing planet. Or the boundary planets in a Bowl or Basket are held in by the nodal axis. This is derived from Vedic astrology and is called Kal Sarpa Yoga which suggests a fated personality; someone who may stand out from the crowd, and indeed, fame may be the spur.

Charts that have Venus and Jupiter as their boundary planets will attract a certain amount of luck and good fortune, while the opposite may be said for Mars and Saturn. In practice, this could indicate help from others with the former, and more self-reliance on the latter, as mentioned before.

If outer planets – Uranus, Neptune and Pluto – are at the boundary, they often propel the individual into world events. Such planets may also be linked to inventors, politicians, scientists or mystics. Mercury and Jupiter acting as boundary planets suggest mental acumen. The Moon and Sun could also propel the person towards the public domain.

The ethos of the planet acting as either one of the boundary planets, handle or singleton blends into the sign and house. Take the planet Neptune for instance. In the chart of George Michael, it is placed in the 5th house, which describes his creativity in songwriting and music, but also his tendency towards recreational drugs. Neptune in the 10th house in the chart of Agatha Christie gave her expertise in poisons, the chief method of execution employed in her murder mystery books. In both charts drugs/narcotics were involved, but with a difference.

When considering an aspect, the slower planet affects the faster one.

There is a tendency when viewing the chart of a well-known individual to look for the signature of what we may know about them; the signature of success usually. After that, there may be confusion as to where to go next. Starting the analysis from chart shapes takes the astrologer to the foundation of the individual's character, the part of a chart which would not normally act as a rallying point. Viewing the chart from its shape may start the analysis from an ostensibly obscure but surprisingly relevant position.

Empty spaces in charts, particularly when no aspect exists across the space, can be more challenging than one where the planets are placed. Often the midpoint of the planets either side of the empty space can be of importance.

Summary

1. **Only judge the shape of chart using ten planets, and ignore Chiron and nodes and aspects, and other points, though bring back these points, or any others, in delineation.**

2. **Look at characteristics of the designated chart shape, positive and negative.**

3. **Dominant element, quadruplicities.**
   How does this support or detract from the basic chart shape?

4. **Boundary planets.**
   Check strength as well as their basic meaning. Are they malefic/benefic, or a mixture?

5. **Leading planet and trailing planet.**
   Distinguish between the boundary planets and compare strengths.

6. **Midpoint of boundary planets.**
   Check by sign, house, aspects and whether linked to planet.

7. **Check significant planets and other planets in normal way. Dignities/debilities, type of houses, quadruplicities, and aspect patterns. See Appendix for further support.**

8. **Singleton.**
   A singleton can be a planet that stands out by virtue of its placement in a different hemisphere, triplicities and quadruplicities. If a handle to a chart is a singleton this has greater strength.

9. **Empty spaces.** The midpoint of the two planets on the boundary of any empty space, whatever the shape, is of importance. Check

if a planet falls/is in aspect to that midpoint. Check also the other midpoints linked to that planet to get a whole view of its real meaning.

10. **The High Focus Planet** (HFP) is different to the planet that has the most dignity in the chart in terms of being in either domicile, exaltation, in a benefic house and so on. The HFP is the one which begins interpretation in any one of the chart shapes, and can either indicate the foundation of personality, or the modus operandi of an individual's life. The HFP should then be judged in terms of dignity and debility.

Notes
* Marc Edmund Jones described the concept of planetary shapes in his book *The Guide to Horoscope Interpretation* (1941). He was born 1 October 1888, 8:37am, St. Louis, Missouri, U.S.A. A writer and screenwriter by profession, he was from an early age interested in the intricate patterns discernable in nature. This led him to develop his distinctive perspectives on astrology. His chart is a Bowl shape with Neptune, the leading planet, linked to vision and imagery, hence the interest in film, patterns and symbols.

** Robert Jansky, detailed his ideas in his book *Planetary Patterns* (1974). He was born 25 October 1932, 5:02am, Hackensack, New Jersey, U.S.A. His early professional life involved biochemical and bacteriological research. His chart might suggest a Bucket shape since Uranus stands on the Western hemisphere, well away from the rest of the planets. Uranus, the handle, is linked to chemicals, and describes the astrologer's early work. However, Jansky did not seem too sure which shape his own chart resembled most!

2
The Splash Shape

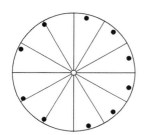

Description

We start with the Splash-shaped chart because it is the pattern that covers much of the chart by planetary placing, then we continue with other shapes as they reduce the field of operations.

In a Splash-shaped chart the planets strive to be evenly scattered around the zodiac, covering a minimum of eight signs, though ten is ideal. Naturally some signs and houses will be empty, but the gap between any two planets should not, ideally, exceed more than 60°, or thereabouts.

If more than one conjunction occurs, this may not be a Splash chart.

This chart shape has been likened to the spokes of a wheel, though with some irregularity – in the chart not the wheel!

There are likely to be a number of oppositions in this type of chart, and the core opposition – between the swifter two planets – may be the best place to begin delineation. This opposition provides the backbone of the chart. The *High Focus* planet is the fastest one within the opposition.

Some astrologers say that the Splash shape may belong to an old or advanced soul, since it would appear that experience has been garnered in many fields, resulting in many talents, with a comparative ease of meeting with other minds. Certainly an individual with a Splash chart endeavours to connect to the Whole: reflecting the idea that we are all connected to the One.

Yet others might argue that the oppositions likely in such a chart could bring tension, strife and challenges into life, indicating further areas of learning which need to be brought into balance. What constitutes an old, or indeed a young soul, may not be determined by shape alone.

Positive Traits

With planets in so many signs/houses, this shape is suggestive of a well-balanced nature or at least an individual with a wide range of interests. Potentially this shape gives an urge to acquire knowledge and information, often leading to a variety of talents.

Thoughts chase around the head like a merry-go-round, and the individual easily goes from one subject/idea to another. Indeed there may be a possibility of reaching a high level of excellence in any field of endeavour spreading ideas far and wide.

There may be an ability to adapt to any situation, and turn difficult circumstances around. Something of a chameleon, this type can switch from one view to another with hardly a pause, keeping a diversity of ideas in mind at the same time.

A marked curiosity is evident which gives flexibility and versatility, with ease and adaptability in new surroundings, even when out of their comfort zone. Good self-expression, with an ability to talk to people on any level, fosters a broad mind, and a willingness to try new ideas.

There always seems to be something happening, with many opportunities. The individual often has a way of circumventing obstacles without recognising boundaries. Striving for order, may look like utter confusion to the outside world.[1]

Challenging Traits

There is a possibility of scattering energies too widely and maybe never achieving excellence in any field. This individual tends to have an opinion on many subjects which can be tedious to his or her listeners. Conversely because of many interests – like a butterfly never staying anywhere too long – this may indicate someone who is difficult to get to know on a deeper level.

With such a flexible mind boredom can easily set in, so new challenges and interests tend to appeal, though there is a threat of not seeing things to conclusion.

Their lives may sometimes look as if in chaos, and can be viewed as a little reckless, as well as a little dissolute, easily distracted, lacking in focus and going off on tangents. There may be a nagging doubt that they haven't achieved very much.

There is little recognition of boundaries, so they may sometimes not know when to call a halt to an enterprise.

Associated Planet: Since the Splash chart tends to give diversity of interest and a life of variety, it seems to accord best with Mercury, the planet of mental acuity and virtuosity.[2]

Example Splash Shape: Dr John Dee, Astrologer

Synopsis

Now mainly remembered as a magician, Dr John Dee was the foremost scholar of his age. His interests lay in alchemy, navigation, astronomy, astrology, medicine, mathematics, writing, and the occult. His search for the Philosopher's Stone as well as his quest for angelic contact was aided by seer, Edward Kelley. What is not so well known is that he was probably the original 007, secret agent. He certainly had an interest in cryptography.

Biography

Dr Dee, who taught classics at Cambridge, thought that the key to understanding the universe rested upon mathematics. He did not see a difference between his occult and scientific interests; to him it was all a pursuit of knowledge. In the 16th and early 17th centuries, the spirit and terrestrial worlds were integrated. It was only at end of the 17th century, known as the Age of Enlightenment, that the occult as well as astrology were relegated to the realms of superstition.

In 1558 Dee fell foul of Queen Mary 1 (Bloody Mary). He was arrested for treason after setting up the monarch's horoscope without permission. This was viewed as spying through magical surveillance. Fortunately, nothing substantial could be proved against him.

His fortunes improved when Elizabeth 1 became Queen, since she supported Dee's work and consulted him on medical matters. He also elected Elizabeth's coronation chart, as most astrologers know. The monarch and the magician corresponded on many secret matters, Dee marking his letters with a double OO with a line above the letters and a line on the right side appearing a little like 007. Could this have been the genesis of the 20th century famous spy of fiction?

Dee's supernatural interests grew over the years and in 1681 he recorded his first angelic conversation. A year later he enlisted the help of Edward Kelley who impressed him with his mediumistic gifts. Dee purportedly used an obsidian mirror (a naturally occurring volcanic glass) for scrying.

Despite his erudition and attendance at court, Dee did not make much money and decided to take up an offer made to him by Polish nobleman Albert Laski to travel to Poland for occult research. He took with him his wife and family, as well as Edward Kelley and family. This venture did not reap great rewards, and Dee spent the next few years travelling through central Europe in the hope of finding a rich benefactor. He was not successful and came back to England.

There he was greeted by a great calamity. His vast library of 3,000 books and 1,000 manuscripts had been pilfered; stolen or sold off, possibly by his brother-in-law who had charge of them during Dee's absence. Many books are now held by the Royal College of Physicians in London.

Astrology

Triplicities
Fire: None
Air: Moon, Uranus
Earth: Venus, Saturn, Pluto
Water: Mercury, Sun, Mars, Jupiter, Neptune

Quadruplicities
Cardinal: Mercury, Sun, Jupiter, Pluto
Fixed: Moon, Mars, Saturn
Mutable: Venus, Uranus, Neptune

Houses
Angular: Uranus
Succedent: Moon, Mercury, Sun, Jupiter, Saturn,
Cadent: Venus, Mars, Neptune

Reception None

Leading Planet None

Boundary Planets None

Singleton Uranus (Angular)

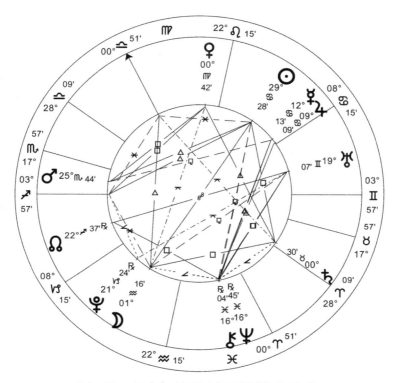

John Dee: 13 July 1527, 16:02 LMT +0:00:40
London, England 51°N30' 000°W10' 16:02

A Splash chart is suggested by the occupation of eight signs, but falling short of the ideal of ten signs. The variety and restlessness inherent in a Splash chart displays Dee's search for the meaning of life, his many interests, and wide travel in an age when travel was rare. Dr Dee's breadth of knowledge was impressive – a corollary of a Splash chart.

The core opposition is between the Sun and Moon, the latter the High Focus Planet – a day after a Full Moon – suggestive of drawing together all levels of consciousness and instructing the masses. The Sun in Cancer desires to build a home or a house of light.[3] In the 8th house the Sun digs deeply behind the veil separating this world and the next. The 8th house is part of the occult triangle along with the 4th and 12th.[4]

The Moon in Aquarius gives objectivity and sees the broader picture. Across the 2nd/8th houses, learning will come through gains and losses. Struggle and hardship follow in cold pursuit as the two planets beckon Saturn into a T-Square. Yet all three planets are on the mid-point of success – Mars/Jupiter at 17.27 Virgo, 9th house. Success in erudition.

Fine scholarship is further suggested by Saturn's trine to Venus, a benefic in the 9th house of higher mind and religion. Venus in Virgo, in its fall, seeks divinity in matter through a practical way, as the magician supposedly did by searching for the secret of the Philosopher's stone. Venus rules the 10th and 6th houses, which drew medical matters into his career. Indeed Dee was particularly interested in exploratory work relating to syphilis, leprosy and gout. A square to Mars brings passion of both a secular and spiritual kind with the warrior strong in Scorpio in the occult 12th house. Enemies abound here too, but a benevolent trine to the Sun gave a way out of difficulties and stayed the executioner's hand.

When there is an aspectual link between the Sun, Saturn and Mars, as there is here, consciousness grows through struggle and strife, and encounters with the dark side. Dr Dee certainly hovered between life and beyond. He saw no differentiation in his studies in mathematics and science as well as the occult, believing all to be part of one creation, which reflects the collectivisation of the 12th house, and the many-sidedness of the Splash chart.

Mercury, the planet traditionally ruling astrology, mathematics and scholarship is associated with the Splash shape, and positioned in the 8th house in Cancer. Here the winged messenger searches for the Divine Plan intuitively.[5] In a cardinal sign Mercury has the drive towards multiplicity of the Splash type, though with Cancer nothing is straightforward.

Mercury gains luck through its conjunction to Jupiter and a touch of telepathy with its trine to Neptune in its own sign, in the 3rd house. Neptune draws in the singleton Uranus in Air with a square. In Gemini, the mind is emphasised once more and both form a T-square with the nodes. This reveals a need to communicate with the gods.

An inconjunct from Pluto to Uranus and North Node completes the picture for investigation into the unknown. Mundanely, Pluto in the 2nd house can show gains and losses in financial fortunes.

The chart is dominated by Water, which strikes the emotional chord, but there is also new life in Water, which Dee sought in erudition and experimentation. The emphasis on succedent houses shows he never gave up.

Example Splash Shape: Ignace Padarewski, Musician/Statesman

Synopsis
In the late 19th and early 20th centuries there was hardly anyone more famous in the field of music than Polish concert pianist Ignace Paderewski. Streets and schools are named after him in many world cities. A star on the Hollywood Walk of Fame in Los Angeles is his too. He even came to greater glory by becoming a Prime Minister of Poland in 1919. After his year's stint in politics, he returned to music and achieved as much success as before.

He received many awards, among them the Legion of Honour from France, and Honorary Knight Grand Cross of the Order of the British Empire (1925).

Biography
Paderewski was born in Poland and graduated from the Warsaw Conservatory in 1878. He was asked to become a tutor of piano at his alma mater, which he accepted. In 1880, Paderewski married Antonina Korsakówna, who died soon after their son was born.

He made his musical debut in Vienna in 1887, and then went on to Paris in 1889 and London 1890, but it wasn't until he played in the United States in 1891 that he achieved his greatest triumph. His name became synonymous with the highest level of piano virtuosity. Success and money brought him homes in Poland, Switzerland and the United States with his own wine groves.

Apart from his superb talent at the keyboard he was extremely charismatic; women swooned during recitals. He was on intimate terms with many crowned heads of Europe, and travelled extensively. His aim was to make as much money as possible so that he could retire and devote his time to composing music, but the millions he made were soon frittered away, though to worthy causes, some of which he did not understand! In his free time he taught himself languages. Besides his native Polish, he could speak quite fluent English, Russian, French, German, and Spanish.

When WWI broke out in 1914, he solicited funds for Poland in the United States. He had a very acute grasp of the political affairs of his land of birth and the world situation generally. Poland had not been a separate country for more than a hundred years and was spliced between Austria, Germany and Russia. When Poland gained her sovereignty after the war, Padarewski was elected President. Most people who met him believed in his sincerity and that he was not seeking power for himself. He was also a signatory of the Treaty of Versailles (1919) on behalf of Poland.

He only lasted one year as President, not because of any fault of his own, except perhaps for having no party. Those darting around the political corridors wanted the surety of a party that would eventually be in power, so were reluctant to further align themselves with him.

Astrology
Triplicities
Fire: Mercury, Jupiter
Air: Venus, Mars, Uranus
Earth: Moon, Saturn, Pluto
Water: Sun, Neptune

Quadruplicities
Cardinal: Moon, Venus
Fixed: Sun, Mars, Jupiter, Pluto
Mutable: Mercury, Saturn, Uranus, Neptune

Houses
Angular: Moon, Venus
Succedent: Sun, Mars, Jupiter, Saturn, Pluto
Cadent: Mercury, Uranus, Neptune

Reception None

Leading Planet None
Boundary Planets None

Singleton None

Paderewski's ability to transcend politics, countries and music reflects the versatility of the Splash chart. His ease of mixing in all circles

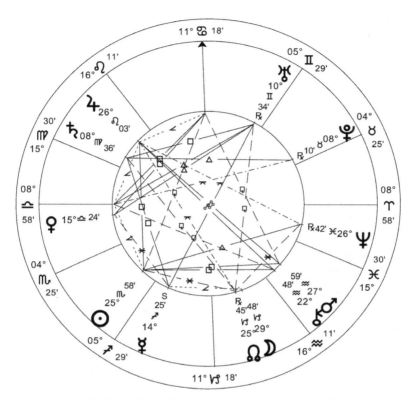

Ignace Padarewski: 18 November 1860 NS 03:00 -1:46:16
Kurylowka, Russia 48°N40' 026°E34'

corresponds with the Splash chart's flexibility. Although his main interest was music, he was fascinated in everything around him, and was an avid reader.

The core opposition is between Mars and Jupiter, which is an adventurous, enterprising energy, demonstrating a willingness to cross frontiers - an echo of the Splash chart. Across Aquarius and Leo respectively, there is an understanding of group ethos and performance, as with 11th and 5th house respectively. Much of Paderewski's success was due to his stage presence, since the 5th is involved in theatricals.

Mars is blighted by a conjunction with Chiron in the 5th house; his only child, a son, was born an invalid and died young. In the house of performance, healing came from his musical creativity. Indeed he had said as much when his first wife died soon after giving birth.

Self-confidence and a positive outlook are brought to bear with these planets in an expansive T-Square with the Sun. Success is assured since all three make a sesquiquadrate and semi-square to the Midheaven. But profligacy with money threatens, since the Sun, the apex of this T-Square, is in the 2nd house.

No doubt the Sun in Scorpio gave him the intensity which characterised all his efforts. Scorpio is a sign of transformation, usually through letting go of past outdated ideas, and often through loss. Sometimes there is a descent into the depths of darkness before the heights of light can be reached. Though successful, Paderewski had his share of sorrow. His mother died a few months after his own birth. The Sun is trine Neptune in Pisces in the 6th house, which indicates sensitivity to the underdog and suffering.

Neptune is sextile the Moon and North Node which highlights his public popularity, especially with women. The Moon in Capricorn shows the ability to stand alone, and without support, not unduly influenced by emotion. Decisions are made without bias. The Moon in detriment can also suggest an emotionally impoverished childhood.

The Moon links to Mercury by a semi-square, a combination giving acute perception. Mercury is linked with the Splash chart. Mercury in Sagittarius, a mutable sign, and in a cadent house, shows his versatility and virtuosity. Since the 3rd is linked with the hands, such elasticity would be helpful to a concert pianist!

Such a supple Mercury must also have contributed to Padarewski's amazing facility for languages, yet it is in detriment in Sagittarius; this to some extent curbs the volatility of Mercury that is now focused upon objectives, for something greater, possibly on universal concepts.[6]

Mercury is also retrograde which creates delays and obstacles in pursuit of plans and education. Paderewski took piano lessons with two private tutors whose teaching was very limited so he taught himself. Mercury went direct 20 days after his birth on 8 December 1860, which corresponded to 1881, counting a day for a year. This is when he began to study in Berlin and released some of his piano compositions.

The slight dominance of mutable planets indicates the ease with which he could turn from one idea or pursuit to another, which is the general message of the Splash chart too. There is enough emphasis on fixed signs and succedent houses to give stability and steadiness of purpose.

Saturn square Mercury was also a steadying influence though being a challenging aspect it brought some trials. Saturn rules the 4th and 5th houses hinting at his impoverished and unsettled early life. The opposition from Uranus in Gemini in the 9th house to Mercury offers talent, even genius, and again the chance to travel. Uranus completes a T-square with Mercury and Saturn, and forms a midpoint with the planets as well. This will show tension and stress upon the nervous system, and indeed, Paderewski could be quite volatile at times. Nevertheless, it probably contributed to his brilliance as an orator.

Mercury sextile Venus, ruler of the Ascendant, suggests artistic/musical talent. Venus is exceptionally strong being in domicile and in the 1st house. He was also known to be an excellent diplomat, which aided his election to the premiership of Poland.

In the natal chart both Fortunes are in aspect to the Midheaven which is a bold signature for success: Venus is square MC, Jupiter semi-square MC.

Drawn to diversity, the Splash shaped chart can nevertheless demonstrate excellence in many areas, though there may sometimes be a feeling of dissatisfaction, of not having achieved enough. In Paderewski's case, his ambition to compose was frustrated because he gave his money away, and couldn't rest on his laurels long enough to follow that dream.

References
1. Jones, Marc Edmund. *The Guide to Horoscope Interpretation*, McKay, Philadelphia, 1941, Quest, 1975, p.9.
2. 'Planetary Patterns in Astrology', Astrotheme.com (11/9/2019).
3. Bailey, Alice. *Esoteric Astrology*, Lucis Press 1951, pp.329, 332.
4. Cornell, H.L. *Encyclopaedia of Medical Astrology*, Weiser, 1933, 1977, p.881.
5. *Esoteric Astrology*, p.323.
6. ibid, p.369.

3

The Locomotive Shape

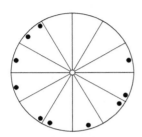

Description

Typically, the planets cover two-thirds of the chart in the Locomotive shape – around 240° – the empty third around 120°, with a trine between the two boundary planets. One planet is referred to as the leading planet, the other the trailing planet.

The leading planet is found by pointing to the empty third of the circle, then moving the eye anti-clockwise towards the nearest planet. No account is taken of the speed of the planet, retrogradation, applying or separating from an aspect except in interpretation. The leading planet prompts the start of action, and analysis. The trailing planet represents the type of ending to be expected, in project terms.

The space between two planets in the two-thirds of the chart should ideally not exceed 60° for the shape to remain a Locomotive.

Although a Locomotive type drives relentlessly towards goals, how they go about it depends upon the nature of the leading planet and its sign and house. A fixed sign will of course, act differently from a cardinal or mutable sign, and if the leading planet is retrograde, then the individual may find obstacles and setbacks litter his path before they can get started.

Since the trine aspects tend to dominate the Locomotive this seems at odds with the drive that is characteristic of this shape. Without a nudge from a square or opposition, the Locomotive may chug away in a pleasant sort of way, achieving goals easily but never quite finding the drive to achieve more. Real power depends upon other aspects to help drive the engine.

Analysis therefore begins with the leading planet in terms of sign, house and aspects, as well as midpoints. The midpoint between the two boundary planets, as well as its sign and house (and that opposite), also symbolises an important focus in the life. Any planet found on this midpoint will be significant in interpretation.

Positive Traits

Versatility as well as adaptability is usually present, like the Splash chart, so the individual tends to connect easily to new people and new surroundings. They are self-reliant and self-motivated, coupled with a clear vision of future possibilities, with confidence usually evident.

Once an idea takes root and the engine starts moving there is usually compulsive energy in carrying out activities, together with resourcefulness in circumventing obstacles – or driving right through them. An ability to see solutions quickly is apparent, indeed they tend to be a good problem solver[1] and persist without tiring until one is found.

Executive ability is often in evidence, with efficient co-ordination[2] giving practical results. This type of chart tends to bestow leadership qualities, possibly with an adventurous, sometimes reckless attitude. Straightforward in approach, sees the objective and goes for it. Carries people along with inspiration and energy by sheer force of personality, even manipulation.

Challenging Traits

The individual with a chart such as this is constantly in motion and may ride roughshod over others, usually through lack of awareness. This can sometimes make them appear callous, self-seeking, even overbearing. Anger can be evident if thwarted in objectives.

They may sometimes act like a bulldozer, clearing everything in their way, which on occasion can overcome seemingly insurmountable obstacles, but there is danger of hurting people's sensitivities. The focused energy can be a little ruthless, self-seeking, and uncompromising.[3]

If there is inability to deal with obstacles quickly, then frustration sets in, and they may suddenly give up, like an engine running out of steam. A lack of support from others may daunt enthusiasm. Despondency does not usually last long though. Fresh inspiration can get things going again, either on the same project, or a different one.

They may not be the best listener so might miss something

important, or only understand half of the matter, so could jump to conclusions, as they are hard to stop once in motion.[4]

Theoretically, the empty houses within the boundary parameters are said to bring problems, or at least the issues featured by those houses may create challenges since the territory is unfamiliar.

Associated Planet: The Locomotive shape appears to reflect the Aries type energy[5] therefore Mars, with its customary focused, sometimes blinkered drive, seems appropriate for this shape.

Example Locomotive Shape: Bobby Fischer, Chess Grandmaster

Synopsis

Bobby Fischer, a United States citizen, was a chess Grandmaster. In 1972 he became the World Chess Champion after beating Boris Spassky of the Soviet Union. At the time it was seen as a Cold War confrontation between America and Russia, attracting interest the world over.

Fischer refused to defend his title in 1975, finding it difficult to compromise with tournament rules. He retired from the world scene for a number of years; he went from world pre-eminence to isolation, and with increasingly erratic behaviour.

In 1992 he entered a rematch against Boris Spassky, and won. When the USA government demanded income tax on Fischer's winnings, he did not return to the country of his birth and settled in Iceland instead.

Biography

Fischer was of Russian, German, Polish and Jewish descent. His parents separated early in his life and he was brought up by his highly intelligent and multi-lingual mother. As a child he always liked games and puzzles, and became interested in chess from the age of six, often playing against himself. From the age of 13 he began to win many championships.

Fischer did not finish his schooling, yet he was able to teach himself several foreign languages so he could read foreign chess periodicals. He eschewed school work even though he had an extremely high IQ, preferring to concentrate on chess. He did so endlessly, working hard with amazing concentration and objectivity when in play. He was charismatic, highly popular but erratic, and could be aggressive. This also brought him many detractors.

At one stage he was a star of the press, but he came to loathe reporters, convinced that they were more interested in sensationalism than writing about chess. It is said he was a loner, despite having many friends and public adulation, yet in order to reach the high level of concentration demanded by the game of chess, much time spent alone is often requisite to attaining excellence. Fischer's single-mindedness about the game concentrated his mind wonderfully, though he enjoyed other pastimes such as tennis and swimming. Religion also played an important part of his life – of a Christian variety – even though he was Jewish. Later in life he became an anti-Semite and a Holocaust denier. He also applauded the terror attack on the twin towers in New York 2001. His behaviour became more and more erratic.

In 2004 he was arrested in Japan for using a passport that had been revoked by the U.S. government due to tax purposes. Eventually, he was granted an Icelandic passport and lived in Iceland until he died in 2008 of kidney failure, refusing treatment. Fischer invented and patented a chess timing system, now standard practice in top tournaments.

Astrology

Triplicities
Fire: Venus, Pluto
Air: Mercury, Mars, Saturn, Uranus, Neptune
Earth: Moon
Water: Sun, Jupiter

Quadruplicities
Cardinal: Venus, Jupiter, Neptune
Fixed: Moon, Mercury, Mars, Pluto
Mutable: Sun, Saturn, Uranus

Houses
Angular: Moon, Venus, Mars, Pluto
Succedent: Mercury, Saturn, Uranus
Cadent: Sun, Jupiter, Neptune

Reception: Mercury/Saturn, Sun/Venus

Boundary Planets: Mars (leading), Neptune (trailing)

Mars/Neptune midpoint: 1.00 Sagittarius in the 5th house – Uranus
    giving great vision but instability

Singleton: Moon (Earth)

This chart is as close as it possible to get to the ideal Locomotive shape. The one-pointed direction assigned to the Locomotive chart and total concentration upon objectives is very pronounced in the self-motivated personality of Fischer, who spent most of his time studying chess. The tendency of the Locomotive to run and run regardless of extraneous events was how he approached life.

Mars as the leading boundary planet, and associated with the Locomotive chart, will magnify the driven and highly-motivated quality

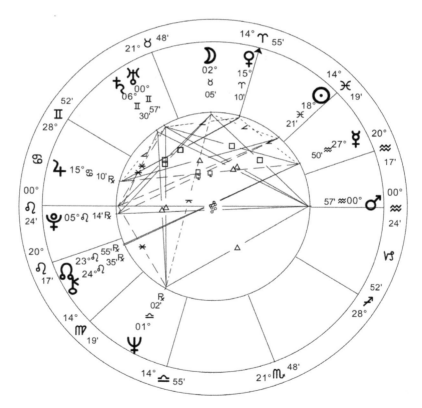

Bobby Fischer: 9 March 1943, 14:39 CWT +5.00, Chicago Heights
41°N30'22" 087°W38'08"

of this shape. The Aquarius placement reflects Fischer's objectivity, as well as his ability to bring together various ideas or aims into a constructive whole, like pieces on a chess board. The fixed quality of Aquarius gives Fischer the patience to ponder chess moves. Indeed the chart is biased towards the Air element and its proclivity to mental acumen, and the ability to visualise chess moves in the mind.

Positioned in a fixed sign, Mars is given stability, and prominence through angularity. In the 7th house, it pits itself against others: the house of relationships and war. Chess is an intellectual game of war – king, queen, castle, knights, soldiers etc. Indeed, Fischer saw himself as a warrior.

Mars rules the MC and 5th house, suggesting a career linked to performance and games of chance. An emotional punch comes from the square to the Moon in Taurus. Fame is suggested by the lunar placement in the 10th house. The Moon is a singleton in Earth and strong by exaltation. However, Fischer could only orientate himself to the mundane through his chosen game.

The Moon and Mars complete a T-square with Pluto on the Ascendant intensifying the power of concentration, compulsive tendencies and charisma. Mars further links into a Grand Trine – usually evident in a Locomotive chart – with Uranus, Saturn and Neptune. The latter is the trailing planet which may slow down the intensity of the warrior. In some circumstances this may not be a bad thing. This Grand Trine can bring vision and force but since Neptune falls on the midpoint of Mars/Uranus, there is a likelihood of overtaxing strength.

Neptune in Libra in the 3rd house gives an almost mediumistic quality to the mind. This could help in forecasting opponents' chess moves.

The boundary planets' midpoint, Mars/Neptune, is 1.00° Sagittarius which falls into the 5th house of games of chance. Uranus is the planet that links to this midpoint by opposition which makes it significant in this chart, bestowing both vision and genius as well as nervous sensitivity. Certainly the former two qualities are helped by a semi-square to the benefics – Venus and Jupiter – as well as a semi-square to the Midheaven and sextile Ascendant.

Uranus in the 11th house indicates involvement in groups: in Fischer's case in large-scale competitions. Uranus conjunct Saturn is likely to bring disputes with team mates, and strain on the nervous system since both are square Mercury. Modern astrological thinking sees Mercury in its exaltation in Aquarius,[6] further emphasising objective and abstract thinking, though compromise may be difficult. Mercury is conjunct the nodal axis. This looks like a genetic link to mental shrewdness, but with Chiron linked to the North Node some kind of mental challenges may be present.

Mercury's sesquiquadrate Jupiter is another sign of mental acumen. Jupiter's trine to the Sun gives good luck. Both benefics, Jupiter and Venus, aspect the Sun. Venus does so by reception by exaltation, suggesting tremendous success on a worldwide level. In the 9th house the Sun is in its Joy, indicating the broad scope of his life, and aids a talent for languages, interest in religions and penchant for travel. Fischer spent much time abroad in latter years. With the Sun sesquiquadrate Pluto, life would keep changing at a fundamental level.

Pisces influencing the 9th house may be indicated in Fischer's renouncement of the world for many years. He may have needed this space to merge with the Divine, or simply to ponder upon his game, alone. After all, the ruler of 9th, Jupiter, is in the isolating 12th house.

Example Locomotive Shape: George Blake, Spy

Synopsis

In 1961 Double Agent George Blake hit the headlines when he was convicted of spying for Russia and given the longest prison sentence in the history of British Justice – forty-two years. A few years later in 1966, he broke out of Wormwood Scrubs prison, skipped across the channel, easily passed through customs, and reached what was then the Eastern Block under Russian domain. He is purported to have betrayed and caused the deaths of many secret agents. One of his most famous betrayals was passing on information about the secret underground tunnel in 1950s' Berlin, running from the American Sector into the Soviet Zone.

Biography

Blake was born in Holland. His father was Egyptian, and his mother Dutch. However, since his father fought for England in WW1, this entitled Blake to a British passport.

Blake's spying took place in the 1950s mainly during the Cold War. He always maintained that his spying was not based on avarice but deeply-held principles, since he abhorred the capitalist cultures of Britain and America.

There is no doubt that George Blake – real name George Behar – led a very eventful life. His father was a shop owner and he died when Blake was 13. His mother, lacking funds, sent him to his father's relatives in Egypt where he acquired a good education and advanced his talent for languages.

Initially he was attracted to the church, but when WW2 broke out, he fought for the Dutch resistance. Later he worked as a British Intelligence officer. He was posted to Cambridge to learn Russian and like many other young intellectuals was attracted to the ideas of communism. It seems he was finally won over to the creed after he had been posted to the British embassy in Seoul, South Korea in 1950, which was subsequently captured. Blake said that it was the bombing by the Americans of the defenceless villagers that had finally turned him to communism. After he returned to Britain, he offered his services to the Kremlin, and became a master spy in the Cold War.

He served two masters up to 1961 when his treachery was discovered. Blake's long sentence was a shock for everyone, both inside and outside of prison, but he seemed to have taken it all in his stride. In fact, he became the model prisoner. Within six years he was out, helped principally by ex-convict Sean Bourke who was bitterly disappointed when they both finally arrived in Moscow. The man he thought was Blake didn't really exist. Only then did he see his ruthless side.

Blake left behind a wife and two sons, as well as a mother and sister but managed to build a new life in Russia, where he is hailed as a hero. To mark his 85th birthday in 2007, he was awarded the Order of Friendship medal by the Russian president, Vladimir Putin.

Astrology

Triplicities
Fire: Moon, Venus, Neptune
Air: Mars, Saturn
Earth: None
Water: Mercury, Sun, Jupiter, Uranus, Pluto.

Quadruplicities
Cardinal: Saturn, Pluto
Fixed: Moon, Mercury, Sun, Mars, Jupiter, Neptune
Mutable: Venus, Uranus

Houses
Angular: Mercury, Sun, Jupiter, Saturn, Pluto
Succedent: Moon, Venus, Mars, Neptune
Cadent: Uranus

Reception: None

Leading Planet: Pluto

Boundary Planets: Pluto (leading), Uranus (trailing)

Uranus/Pluto midpoint: 10.22 Taurus semi-square Moon and Mars

Singleton: Uranus/Cadent

Astrology

A visual glance at this chart supports the Locomotive shape, though it lacks a certain symmetry to be an ideal contender. Nevertheless, it is close enough. There is a trine between the two boundary planets – Uranus and Pluto – cutting off the empty third of the chart. Outer planets in the boundary position often propel the individual into the collective - usually involvement in world affairs.

Blake had the self-reliance and self-motivation that characterises the Locomotive chart, purportedly with a clear vision of life's purpose. There was no doubt that he could ride roughshod over others in his determination to achieve his goals, especially with Pluto as the leading boundary planet. Pluto is concerned with power, death and subterranean themes, all part of Blake's life.

In Cancer and indeed the 4th house, with links to the MC/IC axis, Pluto describes power issues and upheavals in both home and career. The MC is in a wide T-Square with the nodes, ruling alliances[7] and suggesting connections with many people possibly with similar aims on the world stage. In Virgo and across the 6th/12th axis, the nodes do hint at compassion for the underprivileged.

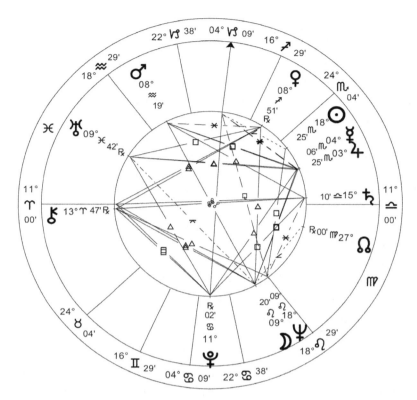

George Blake: 11 November 1922, 15:00 -0:19:32 Rotterdam, Netherlands
51°N55' 004°E28'

The T-Square Pluto makes with Saturn and Chiron across Aries/ Libra, 1st/7th axis suggests tenacity and endurance, as well as facing challenges in his dealings with others. Pluto is easily persuasive with a trine to communicative Mercury, especially as the winged messenger is in Scorpio. Indeed, Pluto trines the Sun and Jupiter in Scorpio, albeit widely, indicating a certain amount of luck in his dealings with others.

The Sun's square to Neptune could create a sense of idealism or being lost in the fog of illusion, for Neptune distorts reality. Blake believed that the agents he betrayed were never killed, which some might say is naïve in the extreme. Certainly espionage is a game of deceit and lies.

The emphasis on Scorpio and the 8th house hints at a struggle between the forces of light and darkness, good and evil, or just opposing sides. This may bring a turning point where the individual encounters severe losses which eventually bring enlightenment and reorientation to a new way of seeing the world.

Mercury and Jupiter, both in Scorpio, are in trine to Uranus, the trailing planet, suggesting a bright, bold and original intellect. Uranus, which strives to better the human condition[8], in Pisces in the 12th house is likely to strive for collective-interelatedness. The midpoint of these two boundary planets Uranus/Pluto is 10.22 Taurus, on which we find the Moon and Mars suggestive of daring, violence and fanaticism.[9] Mars is important because it is the Ascendant ruler and in Aquarius in the 11th house; it drives the individual to fight for the larger issues in life. It is also the planet associated with the Locomotive chart, which in a fixed sign, shows steadiness of purpose.

Mars trine Saturn and sextile Venus suggests calculated charm. Furthermore, Venus together with the Moon forms a Grand Trine with the Ascendant degree which helps to portray a benign exterior. Sean Bourke who masterminded the escape put his own liberty on the line, taken in by Blake's charisma, as he was.

The Moon in Leo tends to give confidence and a need for recognition. This was quite apparent when his treachery to Britain was discovered, since he readily admitted that he had been giving away secrets to the KGB for years. Both Lights are closely linked to Neptune, which might suggest his spiritual inclinations in early life, and a certain saviour mentality that found its outlet in communism, which he thought was the system of belief that would help the world.

References

1.   *The Guide to Horoscope Interpretation,* p.43.
2.   ibid
3.   Jansky, R.C. *Planetary Patterns,* Astro-Analytics Publications 1974, p.42.
4.   ibid
5.   'Patterns in Astrology', Astrotheme.com (2019).
6.   Weiner, Errol. *Transpersonal Astrology,* Element Books, 1991, p.187.
7.   Ebertin, R. *Combination of Stellar Influences,* AFA Inc, 1940/72, p.64.
8.   *Esoteric Astrology,* p.139.
9.   *Combination of Stellar Influences,* p.199.

4

The Bowl Shape

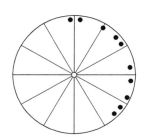

Description

Ideally, a Bowl-shaped chart has the planets placed within 180° of arc, maximum 190°, usually taking up six signs and houses. If less than 130° it's more likely to be a Wedge.

The issues of the tenanted houses are naturally important. The two planets which stand on the border of the Bowl create a Rim Opposition.[1] These are, as mentioned earlier in the book, the boundary planets which are often, though not always, in opposition aspect. If they are, the energy in this chart and individual is more contained.

The planets within the Bowl should, ideally, be less than 60° apart from one another.

The boundary planets, just like the Locomotive, have one that leads and one that trails, but not necessarily with the same one-pointed drive of the Locomotive, rather more steadily, more contained and more contemplative. The leading planet is the planet moving anti-clockwise at the end of the Bowl, referred to as a High Focus Planet. Look at the blank space and move the eye anti-clockwise until hitting upon a planet. This planet is viewed as an important key to the character, together with its aspects, house and houses ruled.

The midpoint pertaining to the boundary planets is of particular importance, and can be judged by its sign and house. Attention is drawn to any planet that may aspect this midpoint by a hard aspect including the half-square and sesquiquadrate. The planet/s in question should be judged along with their other midpoints.

If the nodal line is conjunct the boundary planets, this has special meaning. In Vedic astrology this is known as Kala Sarpa Yoga and whilst it gives many challenges in life, it also has the potential for raising the individual to great heights.

Positive Traits

A strong demarcation line between the individual and the outside world suggests a sense of containment, of being cocooned within safe parameters or a familiar environment. This tends to create a strong focus within designated objectives rather than a narrow life. The interests are usually carried out in depth, and the individual is not likely to be side-tracked.

A strong purpose in life engenders self-reliance. The individual utilises the environment for their own needs, selecting what is most useful, and what is not. The person is usually quite centred and self-aware, works hard towards goals utilising excellent observational qualities. They tend to be a good listener and avidly utilise advice which helps towards achieving their goals.

Energy may be pushed towards a selected purpose with a sense of compulsion that eschews what may be considered superfluous. Ideas are usually put across very well, with an ability to instruct and inspire others.

They tend to hold steady in a crisis, especially if an opposition between the two boundary planets creates a T-square. They are ultimately proficient therefore at taking defensive measures.

Challenging Traits

It's said that there is a lack in understanding or familiarity in the areas of life designated by the empty houses. In a general sense this may be true because the Bowl individual tends to feel more comfortable within a familiar terrain or at least a terrain of his or her choosing, and does not deal well with uncertainty.

The individual may feel reluctant to take up anything new which can seem too challenging, or even threatening. Nevertheless, since there is often curiosity about the world, this may work to their advantage. They are likely to plan well in advance, and become thoroughly familiar with unknown territory. Then they may feel actively challenged in a positive way.

If circumstances occur that force the individual to stray into unknown areas or issues, and they feel out of their 'safety zone', uncertainty and frustration may result, though this gives an excellent opportunity to learn about the needs of others.

A strong directional focus may exist; however, within such parameters there may also be a sense of constraint and even a feeling of imprisonment. Paradoxically, this can also be strengthening and can create leadership in difficult situations. Either much happens in life, or very little, as if just treading water. At times there is a tendency to be a bit one-sided, and a little aloof but this person usually warms up upon getting to know someone.

Associated Planet: The Moon seems a likely candidate to associate with the Bowl not least because of its shape – a half Moon. The Moon also has a containing quality, and looks for safety and security within familiar boundaries. Indeed Jansky suggests the Bowl resembles the Cancerian temperament.[2]

Example Bowl Shape: Arnold Schwarzenegger, Body Builder/Actor/Politician

Synopsis

Arnold Schwarzenegger was born in a small village in Austria and became one of the biggest names on the planet. He was a body-builder – Mr Universe at age 20 – then a high-grossing movie star, author, business man and latterly a statesman.

Since childhood Schwarzenegger was determined to leave behind the relative poverty and strictness of his upbringing. Not only did he fight the limitations of his childhood, he also fought the people who said he would never make it in life, particularly in the movies. His body type, apparently, was no longer fashionable! His name, he was told, was unpronounceable and too long, and his accent unintelligible. Arnold was determined to achieve success on his own terms.

Biography

Schwarzenegger had his sights on the USA since the age of ten; the richest nation in the world which would give him the opportunity to succeed. He worked slowly and surely within the parameters that he set himself, and utilised everything and everyone at his disposal to achieve his aims. He knew what and who he wanted to be. Neither did he want to conform. He studied psychology to see how the mind worked in terms of controlling the body, and decided the way to success was to become a world champion in the body-building world – he never wavered from that goal. He papered his room at home with pictures of body builders who were obviously only clad in shorts, which rather dismayed his mother! He trained daily at the local gym from the age of 15 and when it was closed he even broke in to use the apparatus!

After winning the Mr Universe contest he went on to win the Mr Olympia title seven times. Not only is he regarded as one of the greatest bodybuilders of all time, he also gained worldwide fame as a Hollywood action hero.

He worked unstintingly with tremendous discipline and with a firm eye on his goals. The film that brought him to fame was *Conan the Barbarian* in 1982. Even bigger was *The Terminator* in 1984, where he played a machine in the shape of a human, with no feelings. More highly successful and highly grossing films followed, including a few on the Terminator theme.

Schwarzenegger amassed a great deal of money, married into the influential Kennedy family (Maria Shriver) and entered politics as a Republican. He became governor of California on 7 October, 2003, completing his second term of office on 5 January, 2007. He is also a producer, activist and philanthropist. He was particularly interested in giving children the chance to turn their lives around in deprived areas.

After many years of marriage he is now divorced.

Astrology

Triplicities
Fire: Sun, Saturn, Pluto
Air: Mars, Uranus, Neptune
Earth: Moon
Water: Mercury, Venus, Jupiter

Quadruplicities
Cardinal: Moon, Mercury, Venus, Neptune
Fixed: Sun, Jupiter, Saturn, Pluto
Mutable: Mars, Uranus

Houses
Angular: Mercury, Venus, Neptune
Succedent: Sun, Jupiter, Saturn, Pluto
Cadent: Moon, Mars, Uranus

Reception: None

Boundary Planets: Mars (leading), Moon (trailing)

Moon/Mars Midpoint: 26.49 Pisces in the 10th house –
    Uranus/MC/Saturn/Pluto

Singleton: Moon/Earth

Arnold's chart is a loose Bowl with the Moon and Mars depicting the
two boundary planets. Whilst his sights were set high, Schwarzenegger

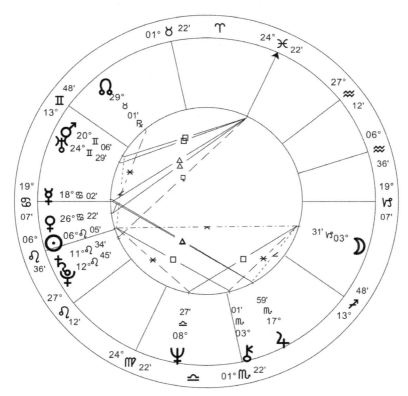

Arnold Schwarzenegger: 30 July 1947, 04:10 CEDT -2:00
Graz, Austria 47°N05' 015°E27'

focused on his ambitions within strict parameters, and a designated terrain, a very wide one – America! He worked steadily towards his goals without wasting time on extraneous pursuits: this is the sense of containment of the Bowl.

Mars, the leading boundary planet, has no dignity in Gemini and is weak in the 12th house, from a traditional viewpoint, therefore a struggle for survival ensues. Mars in Gemini emphasises the mind. Arnold said that the mind is of the most importance in any endeavour, because it is necessary to have a vision to work towards. Mars is given extraordinary energy, as well as originality, by the conjunction with Uranus.

The restriction of the 12th house was expressed in his parents' extremely strict and conventional attitudes, but it fostered discipline. His first goals were self-oriented but since the 12th house is also linked to the collective, he was mindful of giving something back to society. Many charities benefited from his generosity.

Mars and Uranus square the MC indicates drive towards success in unique, original ways, with various changes ensuing. Mars rules the creative 5th house, which suggests a proclivity for performance, as well as the intercepted 10th house, which also indicates more than one career. Uranus rules the 8th house of shared resources, and the ability to change and reinvent oneself.

The tremendous energy of Mars with Uranus was released and further galvanized by the half-square to the Sun – the only aspect – therefore, increasing in importance. The Sun, strong by domicile, cusps the 2nd house, fuelling Schwarzenegger's hunger for success and money (the latter was apparently a secondary aim) nevertheless he achieved both in great measure. The Sun and Mars are on the fortunate midpoint Venus/Jupiter, bringing love, admiration and money.

The emphasis on Leo shows a crisis of individuation and the desire to achieve self-mastery by rising mentally over the environment.[3] This Schwarzenegger certainly did. The Sun achieves more opportunity for financial gain through its conjunction to Venus, discipline with Saturn and power with Pluto.

The trailing planet, the Moon, signifies the public and it is traditionally weak in Capricorn since it is in detriment and constrained in the 6th house. The Moon, a singleton in Earth, is important because it is the planet associated with the Bowl chart. Capricorn is ambitious, aids focus and tends to keep emotions in check. Schwarzenegger did not allow extraneous events to intrude upon his ambitions. Emotional demonstration was largely absent in his early life too.

The Moon, which has links with the functions of the body, garners a need for purification in 6th house, especially since it rules the Ascendant – the body. An interest in health and hygiene ensues, and keeping the body primed by exercise, which Schwarzenegger pursued. This is the house of service, which he may have felt was expressed through his career in politics.

His leading planet Mars and trailing planet the Moon are on the 6th/12th house axis, not known for an easy life or achievement. Having both boundary planets in a challenging position does not preclude success; it is the links such planets make that can reveal triumphs.

The midpoint between the Moon and Mars – 29.49 Pisces – falls into the 10th house, which seems appropriate for such a self-driven individual. Linked to this midpoint are Uranus, Midheaven, Saturn and Pluto which suggest strength as well as violence.[4] Certainly his films did not lack forceful action!

Just as Mars is linked to the strong Sun in Leo, the Moon is half-square fortunate Jupiter in Scorpio in the 5th house. This indicates an ability to change difficult circumstances through enterprise and performance.

Moon square Neptune in the 4th shows possible confusion or secrets linked to the home. There was a rumour that Schwarzenegger's father had been a Nazi during WW2. He arranged for an investigation into his father's background, and found there to be no substance to the rumour. He also lived with a 12-year secret in his marriage; he had fathered a son on his maid, unbeknown to his wife.

The Moon ruling the Cancer Ascendant often indicates the ability to tune into the masses, giving an almost psychic proclivity of what others want. Success shines out with Venus in Cancer in the 1st house. Further towards the Ascendant is Mercury in its Joy, therefore strong, again giving the ability to tune into the masses with a good sense of timing. Mercury and the Ascendant receive blessing from Jupiter with a trine and both Mercury and Ascendant are on Mars/Jupiter midpoint of success at 4.03 Virgo. There is no doubt Arnold is incredibly smart, and a winner.

Cardinal signs have the edge in this chart and show the quality of drive and initiative.

The nodes cut across the chart and seem to contain most of the planets except for the Moon. This is called Kala Sarpa Yoga in Vedic astrology which is said to bring challenges in life but also the possibility of rising to great heights. The ideal Yoga would have all the planets contained within the nodal line.

Example Bowl Shape: Sir Arthur Conan Doyle, Writer

Synopsis

Outside Baker Street tube station in London stands a large statue of the celebrated detective Sherlock Holmes. Just around the corner is his fictional address at 221b Baker Street, now a museum. He almost eclipses his creator, Sir Arthur Conan Doyle, and few are convinced that the erstwhile detective was a fictional character.

'Holmes is the classically divided man that the age (19th century) required: alchemist and rigorous scientific experimenter' xi [5]

His creator, Sir Arthur, trained as a surgeon and wanted to apply science to criminal investigation. He also wanted to investigate spirituality with all the latest technology.

Biography

Conan Doyle had a very unsettled childhood due to his father's delicate mental state. An architect, artist and designer – gifted but unsuccessful, Conan Doyle senior was eventually committed to a mental asylum. However, with the help of the extended family the young Arthur was able to have a good education, studying at Edinburgh University and eventually becoming a doctor. He set up a practice in Portsmouth and began to write stories whilst waiting for patients.

He liked puzzles and problem-solving and in 1886 his interest grew in detective fiction, as well as spiritualism. He was disappointed that most authors did not give adequate clues in their detective novels for the reader to reach conclusions. The first Sherlock Holmes story, *A*

Study in Scarlet (which referred to a message in blood) was published in 1886/87. Here he introduces his detective Sherlock Holmes and his assistant Dr Watson.

Many people now know that the great detective was based on Doyle's professor at Edinburgh University, Dr Joseph Bell, who astounded everyone by his observation in matters of disease as well as in forensic science. Dr Bell laid the foundation for forensic pathology and chose Doyle amongst his students to be his clerk. Conan Doyle found Dr Bell to be distant and cold, which was the norm between teacher and pupil in those days; Sherlock Holmes is cut from the same cloth.

Sir Arthur volunteered his medical services during the Boer War (1899-1902) in Africa where he saw more soldiers and medical staff die of typhoid fever than of wounds sustained in battle. The Great Boer War, a five hundred-page chronicle by Conan Doyle, published in October of 1900, was a masterpiece of military scholarship. It not only reported the war, but was also an astute and well-informed commentary about some of the organizational shortcomings of the British forces at the time. Nevertheless, Sir Arthur was knighted in 1902 for his work,

Conan Doyle was passionate about history and wanted to focus on writing historical novels, but his public clamoured for the detective. Even though the author had at one stage famously 'killed off' Sherlock Holmes, there was such a public outcry that he had to resuscitate him and continue writing more detective novels.

Astrology

Triplicities
Fire: Venus, Saturn
Air: Moon, Sun, Mars, Jupiter, Uranus
Earth: Mercury, Pluto
Water: Neptune

Quadruplicities
Cardinal: Venus
Fixed: Moon, Mercury, Saturn, Pluto
Mutable: Sun, Mars, Jupiter, Uranus, Neptune

Houses
Angular: Mars, Saturn, Jupiter
Succedent: Neptune
Cadent: Moon, Mercury, Venus, Sun, Uranus, Pluto

Reception: None

Boundary Planets: Moon (leading), Saturn (trailing)

Boundary Planet Midpoint: 3.58 Scorpio – Mercury and Mars

Singletons: Neptune/Water, Venus/Cardinal

The Bowl chart emphasises the Eastern side as well at the upper part of the chart, indicating a self-contained individual with a strong inner life. The Moon and Saturn, the boundary planets, indicate a steady and serious personality with a strong sense of duty.

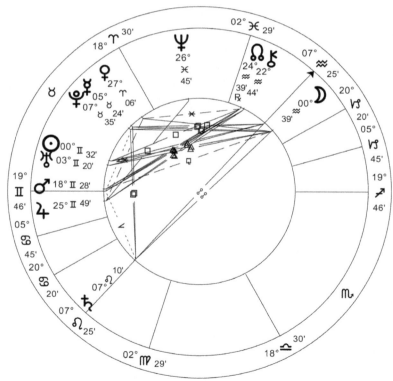

Sir Arthur Conan Doyle: 22 May 1859, 04:55 GMT
Edinburgh, Scotland 55°N57' 003°W13'

The Moon, associated with the Bowl chart, leads in the sign of Aquarius. The observational qualities of the Bowl are also reflected in this sign, evident in Doyle's utilisation of Dr Bell's talents for his fictional detective. Aquarius gives the ability to see all the varying strands that make up the broad picture. A sense of detachment tends towards deduction. The Aquarian humanitarian drives also guided Sir Arthur's life.

The Moon draws attention to the 9th house which rules the higher mind, travel, the law and publishing, all things that were part of Sir Arthur's life. The Moon's closest midpoints are Mercury/Venus and Uranus/Neptune which describe artistic inspiration and mysticism. His interest in spiritualism dominated most of his life; he was a firm believer in reincarnation.

Saturn, the trailing planet, across the MC//IC axis is symptomatic of sadness and difficulty in his early life and problems with the father. Saturn in Leo may well have given him a strong sense of responsibility from an early age. The Moon/Saturn midpoint at 3.58 Scorpio falls into the 6th house, snaring Mars in a sesquiquadrate aspect. Did his father's illness shape his future medical career?

The Moon and Saturn draw in Mercury, Venus and Pluto in a T-Square with the apex in the 12th house which shows a special artistic giftedness and capacity for hard work, toughness and tenacity.[6] Pluto in this interesting cauldron gives a capacity for hard work, and depth of knowledge. Both Saturn and Pluto square and conjunct Mercury respectively adding to Doyle's deep and investigative turn of mind.

The 12th house also hosts the Sun, which disposits Saturn and rules the 4th house of the father. Though incarcerated the Sun receives a trine from the Moon, which might be conjectured that the difficulties of Doyle's early life were dealt with by Sir Arthur fighting for the welfare of prisoners, and miscarriages of justice.

Doyle would use the dark issues linked to his father – addiction, mental illness – in his stories but hardly mentioned them in real life. In *A Study in Scarlet* Doyle's murderer is the thwarted man, a failed artist, a mentally unstable drunk. The compassion and saviour aspect of the 12th house can be seen in the character of Sherlock Holmes' desire to delve into the depths of society in an effort to root out injustice.

The Sun is conjunct Uranus which brings originality, and a scientific quality, echoing the Moon in Aquarius. Uranus has a tendency to create a split in conscious, bringing duality and even more so when positioned in Gemini. The two sides of Sir Arthur: the mystical and the scientific. Neptune's singleton status by element and house contributes to Sir Arthur's interest in psychic matters, but also some might say a tendency towards gullibility.

Gemini is further emphasised by Mars and Jupiter bracketing the Ascendant and therefore creating a very fortunate midpoint. This heralds great success, no doubt helped by Jupiter's sesquiquadrate to the Midheaven. Gemini on the Ascendant gives an understanding that the personality and soul are separate entities, but working towards fusion.[7] Whilst Doyle was quite pragmatic in most things, he did want to know what lay behind the veil between life and death.

References
1.   *Planetary Patterns* p.7.
2.   ibid p.10.
3.   *Esoteric Astrology* p.310.
4.   *Combination of Stellar Influences* pp.98-99.
5.   Conan Doyle, A. *A Study in Scarlet*, 1887, Penguin 2001, Introduction by Iain Sinclair, p. xi.
6.   *Combination of Stellar Influences* p.146.
7.   *Esoteric Astrology* p.368.

5

The Bucket Shape and its Variations

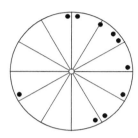

Description

The Bucket shape – sometimes called Basket – is like a Bowl shape, but one planet is placed some distance from the rest and referred to as the handle. The ideal Bucket shape has nine planets in one hemisphere or in a 180° of arc though this can be stretched to 190°, with the handle around 90° from the boundary planets.

The distance between any two planets in the Bowl part should be less than 60°.[1] The lone planet or handle, sometimes also called a Funnel, channels the planetary energy in the Bowl part of the chart.

If the handle planet is directly above the centre of the bowl, this is considered highly focused energy, especially if the handle is in opposition to a planet within the centre of the bowl. There is very definite ambition and single-mindedness.

The Bucket chart, which works within close parameters, is supported by the two boundary planets, which have a bearing on the personality and life of the individual. This becomes more pronounced if the midpoint of the boundary planets falls on the handle planet, or if another planet in the chart is linked to the boundary planets' midpoint.

Positive Traits

The Bucket chart does not quite have the containment of the Bowl chart since there is greater willingness to deal with matters that originate outside of the boundary parameters and reach into the unknown. Unlike the Bowl chart it is not quite so interested in conserving its resources.[2] Nevertheless, the individual with this shaped chart aligns himself to where efforts count most. The focus of activity is within the hemisphere containing the planets, with eventual expression through the handle planet.

The handle, usually the High Focus Planet, emphasises self-projection, and possibly single-mindedness, a compulsive drive and inspired ideas. In the unoccupied area of the chart, it scoops up experience and brings it to the Bowl area where it is examined and integrated.

The handle is also referred to as a 'cutting planet', which slices through the invisible boundary line between the boundary planets, the latter suggesting areas of interest and challenge. This brings a relationship between the boundary planets and the handle planet, almost like a midpoint. If the handle planet is closer to the leading boundary planet, then the individual is more cautious; closer to the trailing planet, then more adventurous.

The Bucket chart may be characterised by a T-square or Grand Cross, which gives more challenges, and possibly greater strength, with definite ambition and single-mindedness.

Challenging Traits

The planet representing the handle acts as a feeler in the part of the chart area which may appear unfamiliar in worldly terms, so whilst this acts as an exciting challenge, it may also feel insecure and a little uncomfortable.

Unfamiliarity could bring a slightly aloof or uncompromising attitude[3], usually because untried ideas can feel a little unsafe. This might acquire the individual a reputation as an agitator, especially in very new territory. Though this may upset the apple cart in certain circumstances it can create new conditions of interest.

Associated Planet: Jupiter. The handle is like the arrow of the centaur, or the thunderbolt of the god Jupiter. How strong the thunderbolt or arrow may be depends on planet, sign and house. (This includes the variation: Sling, Conjunction and Two Handles).

Example Bucket Chart: George Michael, Singer, Songwriter

Synopsis

George Michael was one of the fastest selling artists in the latter decades of the 20th century, first with Andrew Ridgeley in the band Wham, then as a solo artist. He was good looking, charismatic and a very talented singer-songwriter.

With fame and money came the exciting and wild life of a rock star. He admitted to having many lovers of both sexes before he finally accepted that he was gay. In later years he almost wanted to give his money away, feeling he had made enough, and in fact became a very generous benefactor of good causes.

Biography

The singer of Greek/English origin was raised in London. He found out later in life that he also had a Jewish maternal grandmother, who had kept it secret because of her fears in WW2.

From childhood he dreamt of being famous; the money was of secondary consideration. He certainly achieved his goal. He had six hit singles before he was twenty-six, all of which he wrote, sang and produced. He was driven, hardworking, proud and yet had a great deal of humility. The singing duo with school friend Andrew Ridgely claimed such hit singles as *Wake Me Up Before You Go-Go*, and albums such as *Faith*.

The iconic *A Different Corner* was a solo hit just before he decided to break up Wham and become a solo singer. Despite his global success with his former partner he had misgivings about going it alone, yet he became one of the best selling artists of all time.

Michael finally came out as gay in 1998 and became a campaigner and HIV/AIDS charity fund-raiser.

His death is recorded as a disease of the heart muscle (dilated cardiomyopathy), which becomes stretched and thin. It can be an inherited condition or triggered by viral infections, uncontrolled high blood pressure and excessive alcohol consumption.

Astrology

Triplicities
Fire: Moon, Jupiter
Air: Mercury, Venus, Saturn
Earth: Mars, Uranus, Pluto
Water: Sun, Neptune

Quadruplicities
Cardinal: Sun, Jupiter
Fixed: Moon, Saturn, Neptune
Mutable: Mercury, Venus, Mars, Uranus, Pluto

Houses
Angular: Jupiter
Succedent: Neptune
Cadent: Moon, Mercury, Venus, Sun, Mars, Saturn, Uranus, Pluto

Reception: Sun/Moon

Boundary Planets: Mars (trailing), Saturn (leading)

Mars/Saturn Midpoint: 2.08 Sagittarius/5th house – Jupiter/Uranus/Asc

Singletons: Jupiter (Angular), Neptune (Succedent)

Handle: Neptune

In this Bucket-style chart, Neptune represents the handle, and becomes the High Focus Planet. It struggles in the depths of Scorpio to find the beauty within, which expresses itself through the creativity of the 5th house: writing, music and performance in Michael's case.

Neptune in the empty space of the chart reveals how Michael aspired tentatively towards a new area of creativity in his career, since Neptune also co-rules the Midheaven. Success comes from Neptune's Grand Trine with the MC as well as being on the Mars/Jupiter midpoint of achievement. Neptune gains strength by being a singleton, the only planet squarely in a succedent house, suggesting persistence and longevity, at least in his career.

Neptune as the handle is also termed the 'cutting' planet as if it might cut through the boundary planets, creating a relationship for good or ill. With the malefics Mars/Saturn on the boundary, this

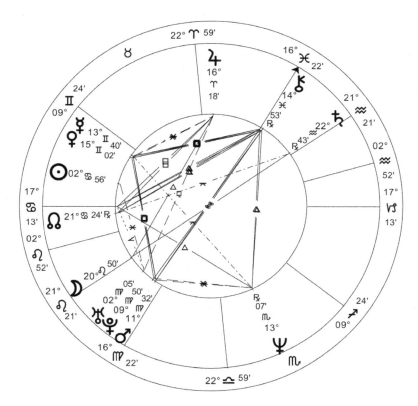

George Michael: 25 June 1963, 06:00 BST -1:00
Finchley, England 51°N36' 000°W10'

threatens torment, depression and loss[4], all which he experienced. These hard planets can also give a certain amount of grit.

Saturn in Aquarius, in the 9th house, develops a strong sense of group consciousness, which found expression through charitable works. However, conflict with the media and the law was always threatening through the opposing Moon in Leo, on the cusp of 3rd house.

No doubt the Moon's position helped with his magnetic presence on stage, and natural ability for leadership. The Moon rules the Cancer Ascendant which reflects the masses. On 3rd house cusp, where it has its Joy, it bestows creative imagination, though mood swings may arise. The Moon's mutual reception with the Sun creates a strong link with the public. However, lack of grounding may come with the 12th house Sun since within this area the line of demarcation is shaky between this world and the next – hence the reclusive qualities of the 12th house. The older George wanted to inhabit less of the world, i.e. publicity or performance. Drugs and drink can often act as a balm to the harshness of the world; always a possibility with strong 12th house and emphasis on Neptune.

Neptune is sextile the other boundary planet Mars, which turns the imagination into a driving force in the career, since it is conjunct the IC/MC axis. Together with Uranus and Pluto in Virgo in the 3rd house, this lifts communication on to a higher level; indeed George had the amazing ability to make up songs in his head. There could be a tendency towards anxiety, even self-doubt. Leaving Wham for instance and going solo was a nerve-wracking decision.

Mars opposes Chiron on the 10th house cusp, which shows a wound linked to the family, and to his self-image. In youth he thought himself unattractive and fat, though he was to become greatly loved and adored by millions. But family skeletons were not far away. The actual midpoint made by Mars and Saturn at 2.09 Sagittarius, draws in the Ascendant and Jupiter by sesquiquadrate and Uranus by square. In summary, this suggests inhibitions, separation, mourning and bereavement. On or close to the day George was born his maternal uncle committed suicide, ashamed of being gay, it seems.

Nevertheless, the link between Jupiter, Uranus and the Ascendant does make for sparkling success. Jupiter in Aries, a singleton through angularity, indicates an ability to lead the way and rely on his own abilities, hence his urge to go solo. Jupiter ruling the Midheaven and sextile Venus brings two Fortunes together, sparking great success.

Venus is conjunct Mercury in Gemini, a signature of artistic acumen. Here in the 12th house Venus looks for its highest expression of love, which may turn towards religion or spirituality. George himself has said that through love we are searching for a glimpse of the divine.[5]

Mercury and Venus create a T-square with the Midheaven and Mars giving power and drive to creativity. All his expressive feelings and qualities were ultimately filtered through Neptune, the handle to the Bucket, into writing and performing.

Example Bucket Chart: Mata Hari, Dancer and Spy

Synopsis

Mata Hari, a name synonymous with espionage and seduction, was shot by the French in October 1917 as a spy during WW1. The war was going badly for the Allies, and it is possible they needed a scapegoat because declassified files by the British, French and even the Germans show very little evidence of her guilt. It is quite possible that she was just caught up in monumental events and became a victim of circumstance.

Judging by her immense popularity as a dancer, and abundant amorous conquests, she was extremely charismatic. Mata Hari had reached the pinnacle of her fame as an exotic dancer during La Belle Époque, (c.1871 to outbreak of WW1) a time of great scientific, technological and artistic advancement in France and Europe.

Biography

Mata Hari was born Margaretha (Margreet) Geertruida Zelle in Leeuwarden, Holland. In a country where everyone was fair, she stood out with her black hair, brown eyes and olive skin. A wealthy and comfortable family life was brought to an abrupt end when her beloved father lost his money and deserted the family. Her mother died soon after, and Margreet and her siblings were farmed out to relatives.

With no money of her own, she married a Dutch Colonial Army Captain, Rudolph MacLeod of Scottish descent in 1895. She went to live with him in Indonesia, and had two children, a boy and a girl. Unfortunately he was alcoholic and violent, and she left him.

In 1905 Margaretha retrained as a dancer, and changed her name to Mata Hari (eye of the day in Javanese). She simulated Indonesian dance traditions and fame came swiftly. The excellence of her dance might have been questionable but not her considerable magnetism – men simply adored her. The fact that she appeared to dance naked also had its attractions. She actually wore a body stocking and her breasts were covered by a bejewelled metal bra.

A life on the stage brought wealthy connections, and as she grew older, she relied more on financial support from relationships with important men, particularly high ranking military officers. Although her native country Holland remained neutral in the Great War, her liaisons with German as well as French military men created a reputation for her as a dangerous woman.

Fraternization with the enemy was seen as spying, as was her fluency in languages and extensive travel. On 13 February 1917 the French arrested her on suspicion of spying for the Germans. Incarcerated in the Saint-Lazare prison for women, her cell was dark, dirty and devoid of sanitary conditions. Mata Hari strongly denied her guilt.

The most incriminating evidence was her own admission that she had taken money from the Germans, but denied ever passing on information. (They had earlier confiscated valuable possessions so she felt they owed her). She might have been deliberately framed by the Germans who used a cipher they knew the French had already broken.

In Holland there is a bronze statue (by Suze Berkhout) of Mata Hari in dancing costume outside the house where she was born in Leeurwarden. Shakespeare said that the evil men do lives after them,[6] and indeed, Mata Hari's name might have remained only a footnote in dance history had she not been shot as a spy.

Astrology
Triplicities
Fire: Mercury, Sun, Mars, Uranus
Air: None
Earth: Neptune, Pluto
Water: Moon, Saturn, Venus, Jupiter

Quadruplicities
Cardinal: Venus
Fixed: Mercury, Sun, Mars Jupiter, Uranus, Neptune, Pluto
Mutable: Moon, Saturn

Houses
Angular: Moon, Jupiter, Saturn, Pluto
Succedent: Venus
Cadent: Mercury, Sun, Mars, Uranus, Neptune

Reception: None

Handle: Jupiter

Boundary Planets: Saturn (leading), Uranus (trailing)

Saturn/Uranus Midpoint: 28.06 Taurus – MC & Venus

Singleton: Venus/Cardinal/Succedent

The Jupiter handle in Scorpio in the 1st house indicates personal success and magnetism, amplified by its opposition to Pluto in Taurus across the horizon. Her appetites, as well as her conquests, were legion, not to mention meetings with moneyed and influential people on a huge scale, although with Pluto in the 7th house power struggles threatened.

The foregoing opposition forms a T-square with the planets in Leo, including Mars, traditional ruler of the Ascendant. Scorpio rising can indicate a life of struggle, and challenges in the sphere of sex, power

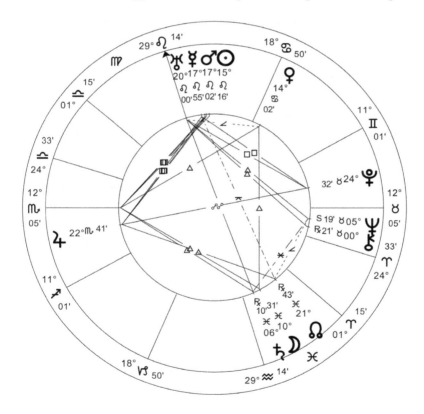

Mata Hari: 7 August 1876, 13:00 LMT - 0:23:04
Leeuwarden, Netherlands 53°N12' 005°E46'

and resources. Mars conjunct the strong Sun – in its own sign and in its Joy – contributes to sexual magnetism and active self-promotion.

Mars conjunct Mercury gives sharpness of intellect – she was very quick witted. Mars rules the 5th and 6th houses proposing a penchant for pleasure and entertainment as well as children and health issues. A son died through poisoning, it seems, and a daughter was taken from her.

Uranus, the planet of innovation and originality, completes a quadruple conjunction in Leo and close to the Midheaven influences her career, which brings fortune since Uranus is on the midpoint of success – Mars/Jupiter. The emphasis on the 9th house suggests wide experiences, namely travel, fluency in languages, intelligence and contact with the law. Maybe a spiritual quest too. Mata Hari's dance was spiritually based but sexualised, a heady combination.

Leo being so prominent suggests strong individuality. Certainly Mata Hari was determined to tread her own path in life. The prominent Sun's rulership of the 10th house of career contributes to her phenomenal success, helped along by the fixed star Regulus on the MC which tends to lift the individual to the dizzy heights of fame. Fame came quickly after her dancing debut on 13 March 1905 at the Musée Guinet in Paris, her adopted city.

The vibrant planetary placing in Leo contrasts against the somewhat dour combination of planets in Pisces, which rather sums up the life of Mata Hari: she rose to great heights and plummeted to the lowest depths. The Moon and Saturn in Pisces show a tendency towards victimisation, which she suffered at the hands of her violent husband, and eventually the French government. Saturn, Moon and North Node in Pisces – 4th house – indicate restriction and victimisation at end of life (prison).

With Saturn as the leading planet there is a need to face the music in this lifetime so to speak, or karmic obligations, and she did face them with aplomb; it's rumoured that she even blew a kiss to the firing squad. Quite believable with the Moon trine Venus, as both planets remain popular with the public even if they are holding weapons of destruction.

Venus, a singleton and the only planet in cardinal signs and succedent houses certainly has the ability to draw the public, especially throwing a trine to the Ascendant. In Cancer, Venus has a maternal quality and the only time Mata Hari fell in love was with a penniless Russian soldier almost half her age. She wanted to give up her life as a courtesan but needed money to look after him. Note Venus in the 8th house has association with transformation and death, and indeed it was whilst travelling to her lover through war-torn Europe in 1916 that the path to her downfall was set.

Feelings are paramount with the emphasis on Fire and Water, with active connections arising from the prominent Western hemisphere. Both the boundary planets – Saturn and Uranus – rule her 4th house, the leading and trailing planets respectively. Despite inauspicious beginnings she achieved great success, and the auspicious Uranus midpoint meant she will be long remembered.

The Bucket Chart: Sling Variation

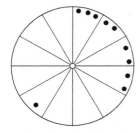

Description

This a more condensed form of a Bucket/Basket shaped chart, where nine of the planets are concentrated in an area of 120°, except one (or maybe a conjunction of two planets), which stand opposite the main planetary group.

Like the Bucket chart, the planet which acts as a handle – sometimes called a Funnel – is the focal point of the chart through which the energies of the main body of planets are channelled. The true Sling has a tightly packed main group of planets. Some versions are a little looser which creates more adaptability.

The handle does not have to be directly opposite the cluster of planets, but should at least be 60° degrees away from one of the boundary planets. However, interpretation will differ: the closer the handle is to the main body of planets, the greater tendency towards collaboration with others. Aspects and midpoints to the handle planet spearhead interpretation.

Boundary planets should also be considered in interpretation, as well as their midpoint. It is thought that the house opposite to the midpoint in the open area holds the key to the personality, or at least is a strong focus for interpretation. But both houses are equally important.

If the main grouping of planets is within a span of 90° this may fall under another shape, a variety of the Wedge (Bundle) chart called a Fanhandle.

Positive Traits

This can indicate a determined, very resolute individual who may feel that he or she is destined for something in life. Since they tend to know a lot about one particular area in life, this might be possible. The person is a pugnacious fighter, acts like a spring and is not afraid to take on challenges that appear almost insurmountable as in the proverbial Bible story of David and Goliath.

They tend to go straight for the jugular, right to the core of any subject and are likely to force issues using all necessary resources to do so. Self-determination and self-belief may be characteristic of this type who may well stand apart from others, with a belief in their special destiny. They could be very charismatic.

Challenging Traits

This individual tends not to take life lightly, being passionate about their beliefs and they may swing to extremes. Convinced they are right in whatever they do results in someone who takes a sledgehammer to crack a walnut. Indeed, they may hit back precipitously without thinking things through. There is a possibility that he or she may be narrow-minded in their determination to achieve. Sometimes in leaving people behind they may end up feeling like an outsider.

Associated Planet: Jupiter, like the thunderbolt that the mythological Jupiter wields, tends to go straight towards its aim which can be just the right thing to do, or can mess up the situation.

Example Sling Chart: Sir Humphry Davy, Scientist

Synopsis

A giant in science, he came to fame by devising a safety lamp for miners that would light the collieries without causing explosions, which had previously been a frequent occurrence, causing many deaths.

Using the new phenomena of electricity Davy broke substances apart to reveal previously unknown elements such as sodium, potassium, barium, strontium, calcium, boron and magnesium. The Prince Regent made him a baronet and the Emperor Napoleon awarded him a medal for his scientific work, even though France was at war with England at the time!

Biography

Davy's story is very much a tale of rags to riches. He reached the heights of fame through his intellect, talent and abilities, although he was born into a poor family and was basically self-taught. His schooling was negligible but he was a voracious reader, and acquired a great deal of knowledge.

Apprenticed to a surgeon, he had the good fortune to meet two further surgeons who had scientific backgrounds, Gregory Watt and Tom Wedgwood.

In 1798 Davy was given a post at the Medical Pneumatic Institution in Bristol, where much of his understanding of scientific inquiry and the role of the inquirer was shaped. It was here that Davy discovered nitrous oxide, better known as laughing gas, as he coined it. The gas has more serious applications however: it is both an anaesthetic and analgesic and has been used in surgery and dentistry, but at the time of discovery it appeared to be used as a recreational drug, as well as a tool for expanding consciousness.

Davy had a strong poetic streak and his friends numbered several poets, such as William Wordsworth, Robert Southey and Lord Byron. All were eager to try the 'laughing gas'.

Davy joined the Royal Society, where he associated with the elite and began to establish a name for himself. He later became President of the society.

His work with electricity seemed to 'unlock' the secrets of life. In his lectures at the Royal Institution he was able to explain lucidly, and show by experimentation, the basis of his theories. At one point he burnt diamonds – hardest of all natural substances – to show that they were made of the same substance as coal, that is, carbon. (The two substances differ in their atomic bonding)

It is quite possible that Mary Shelley – who in her book had Frankenstein's monster spark into life through an electric thunderbolt – had been influenced by Davy's work.

Davy was knighted in 1812, and in the following year he travelled to France with his wife and new assistant Michael Faraday, who was also to become a leading light in the electrical field. In France, Davy demonstrated the elemental status of a new substance he named iodine, but became involved in disputes with French chemists. Davy and his party went on to Italy, where his famous experiment with diamond took place. He took time off to climb Mount Vesuvius and began to develop a theory of volcanism.

Astrology

Triplicities
Fire: Moon, Sun
Air: Mars, Uranus, Neptune, Pluto
Earth: Mercury, Venus, Jupiter,
Water: Saturn

Quadruplicities
Cardinal: Mercury, Venus, Mars, Neptune
Fixed: Saturn, Pluto
Mutable: Moon, Sun, Jupiter, Uranus

Houses
Angular: Moon, Jupiter, Saturn, Uranus, Neptune
Succedent: Mercury, Venus, Sun, Mars
Cadent: Pluto

Reception: None

Handle Planet: Uranus

Boundary Planets: Jupiter (leading), Pluto (trailing)

Jupiter/Pluto Midpoint: 28.18 Scorpio

Singleton: Saturn (Water), Pluto (Cadent)

Davy threw himself with gusto into everything he did, determined to meet the challenges that came his way, so very typical of the Sling-shaped chart. The handle, Uranus, is tailor-made for a scientist, since this planet is linked to chemistry, electricity as well as science.[7]

Uranus in Gemini suggests an agile, original mind spurred on by the trine to Mars. On the cusp of 8th house of hidden phenomena, he uncovered laws of science which may well have seemed like magic to most people in his day. His experiments were often quite dangerous –

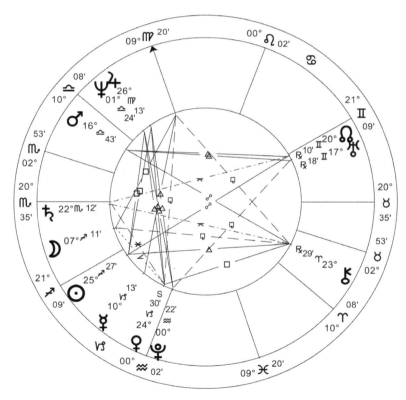

Sir Humphry Davy: 17 December 1778, 05:00 LMT + 0:22:12
Penzance, England 53°N12' 005°E46'

he had the courage to dice with death – and on one occasion nearly blinded himself.

His colossal intellectual energy seems well represented by the sesquiquadrate aspect Uranus makes to Pluto in Aquarius in the 3rd house of lower mind. Pluto's singleton status gives it further prominence. Uranus inconjunct singleton Saturn, albeit widely, in Scorpio on Ascendant promises grit, determination and effort. He had to rely on himself to attain an education. It all came good because both Saturn and the Ascendant are on the midpoint of success, Mars/Jupiter.

A further aspect to Uranus – the handle planet – involves the conjunction to the Moon's Node giving a connection with the populace, and alliances with scientists. The nodes draw Uranus into an opposition with the Sun indicating originality far-sightedness and curiosity. The Sun and Uranus both rule Light[8] which is what fascinated Davy.

Neptune influencing the Sun with a square also has a connection to Light, as well as poetry. Links to the outer planets can connect the individual to the collective, and possibly originality. The square from Jupiter to the Sun shows his desire to push through boundaries. In detriment, and ruling the 4th house, it reflects his lowly birth. Jupiter linked to the Sling chart is however in the 10th house, which ultimately helped Davy's rise to fame, and being in Virgo it was through practical experimentation.

Further, both the Sun and Moon in Sagittarius show far-sightedness. There was no doubt that he travelled far both in body and mind and was always mindful of future possibilities. Due to his inventions Davy was very well known all over Europe.

He was born the day before a solar eclipse, which often heralds an extraordinary individual. The Sun in the 2nd house assumes an accumulation of wealth, and indeed, that is what happened. With the Sun square its ruler, Jupiter, money was likely to come his way. This house can also bring spiritual illumination and the secret of light if we correlate it with the sign of Taurus.[9] The light Davey devised for miners might well have been a physical expression of things spiritual, expressed by saving many lives the world over.

The 2nd house is further emphasised by containing Mercury and Venus in Capricorn. The winged messenger now aspires towards achievement of some higher objective. Mercury is in trine to the MC indicating ease of communication, and indeed Davy was a mesmerising speaker. Otherwise Mercury is unaspected, and this might suggest that there is no limitation to the flight of thought. In modern colloquial terms he thought outside the box.

Venus in Capricorn also shows a calm, steady mind that looks for the truth and is not overcome by emotion, which is helpful for experiments, as is the trine to Jupiter, the leading boundary planet, traditionally also planet of science.[10] The boundary planets, Jupiter and Pluto, are linked to the handle Uranus and describe the reformist tendencies that were so typical of Davy.[11]

The Bucket Chart: Conjunction Handle Variation

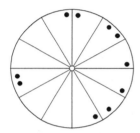

Description

Eight planets reside within 180° (maximum 190°) of arc, ideally in six houses, which may be placed across the traditional hemispheres: East, West, North, South, or cut across them. The handle will contain a conjunction in the opposite hemisphere. It is suggested that the closer the conjunction, the more powerful it is.

The two planets in conjunction must be at least 60° from the main body of planets, though the ideal is around 90°. If there is an opposition between the lone conjunction to a planet in the main body, this is of importance in delineation. It can be said to be the core opposition. Nevertheless, all planetary aspects to the handle conjunction are of importance.

Further, a T-square including the two boundary planets is usually a vital key to character. If one does not exist, the two boundary planets are still important but there is not necessarily the same intense focus or containment; since the individual is more adaptable. Quite often a Grand Cross characterises this type of chart.

Midpoints to the handle conjunction should be considered.

There is a view that a chart that has even two planets opposite the other eight should be considered a See-Saw. No doubt the qualities of a See-Saw chart may be taken into consideration, but some feel a true

See-Saw should have a minimum of three planets opposing the other group of planets.

Positive Traits

There seems to be a need to align oneself where efforts count most, with significant planning ahead. The focus of activity is within the hemisphere filled with planets, though the energy is funnelled through the handle conjunction. Whilst there may be a strong demarcation line between the individual and the outside world, this can be breached by the handle planets.

There tend to be periods spent in relative seclusion, and then periods of exploration, but always with a strong foundation of security. There is usually excellent knowledge in certain areas, with the utilisation of the environment for own needs.

Challenging Traits

Though there is strong focus, with an ability to work within narrow confines, there may also be a sense of constraint, a feeling of limitation. In some cases however, circumstances arise which force the individual to face certain challenges within those limitations.

Quite possibly, this individual is not likely to take advice from others, preferring to be guided by own ideas. There may however, sometimes be a sense of isolation. Either much happens in life, or very little, just treading water.

The empty spheres can show a sense of insecurity, and a reluctance to take on anything new unless such unknown areas are thoroughly investigated beforehand.

Example Bucket Conjunction Variation: Agatha Christie, Crime Novelist

Synopsis

Crime mystery writer, Dame Agatha Christie, is according to the *Guinness Book of Records*, the best selling novelist of all time, after Shakespeare and the Bible. Translated into many languages, her body of work was huge comprising novels, plays, short stories and poems, many including the iconic characters Hercule Poirot and Jane Marple.

The longest-running play of all time – *The Mousetrap* – is a product of her pen.

Having worked in a pharmacy during both World Wars she had a good knowledge of poisons, which became the murder tool of choice – in her books of course. Less well known is the fact that under the pseudonym Mary Westmacott she also wrote six romances.

Biography

Agatha was born in Torquay to an affluent family, and many of her books are set amongst the moneyed classes. She taught herself to read before being tutored at home. Free therefore to use her imagination without the trammels of a conventional education, she explored the world about her with her extraordinarily curious mind, and a huge appetite for learning.

Her mother and sisters had a flair for writing but Agatha was more interested in music and mathematics – in fact, she wanted to be a concert artist but soon realised that she was much too shy to perform in public. She rather liked puzzles and her books are like unravelling some mystery, always to do with murder.

At age 11 her father died and then money troubles began. A good number of her books had money as a motive for murder. Her first detective story – *The Mysterious Affair at Styles* – was published in 1920. She had a long career, worked hard to make the books appear easy, loved to travel, buy houses and swim and surf.

Very attractive as a young girl she had many suitors, settling finally for WW1 flying ace Archibald Christie. Blessed with one daughter, she thought the marriage was a success until in 1926 Archie asked for a divorce to marry a younger woman, a golfing companion. Years later she used the sport as a setting in one of her murder mysteries – *Murder on the Links.*

Archie did not leave immediately, and one night after quarrelling, he set off for a weekend with his mistress. Agatha left home the same night and disappeared without trace for eleven days, sparking a nationwide hunt. Her disappearance remains a mystery, and she does not mention it in her autobiography. Various theories suggest a nervous breakdown, an act to punish her husband or indeed a publicity stunt. In fact, it may not have been a mystery at all. She apparently wrote to her brother-in-law saying where she would be but he mislaid the letter. Nevertheless, her fame certainly grew after this episode.

The Christies finally divorced in 1928. Her second marriage, to archaeologist Max Mallowen, was very happy. He wrote academic tomes on archaeology, and she considered him the real writer in the family, not herself. However, it was she who brought in the money. Some of her books are set in the middle-east and on archaeological digs.

Astrology

Triplicities
Fire: Mars
Air: Moon, Mercury, Jupiter Uranus, Neptune, Pluto
Earth: Sun, Saturn
Water: Venus

Quadruplicities
Cardinal: Moon, Mercury, Uranus
Fixed: Venus, Jupiter
Mutable: Sun, Mars, Saturn, Neptune, Pluto

Houses
Angular: Mars, Saturn, Neptune, Pluto
Succedent: Moon, Mercury, Sun
Cadent: Venus, Jupiter, Uranus

Reception: Mercury/Saturn – Exaltation

Handle Planets: Neptune/Pluto

Boundary Planets: Saturn (leading), Jupiter (trailing)

Jupiter/Saturn Midpoint: 20.55 Scorpio/3rd/4th

Singletons: Venus/Water, Mars/Fire

Agatha's chart leans towards a Bucket type with handle Neptune/Pluto in conjunction, yet there is also a suggestion of a Locomotive shape due to the trine between Jupiter and Neptune. In either case, Neptune remains the High Focus Planet.

A handle comprising Neptune/Pluto is suggestive of life tuned into

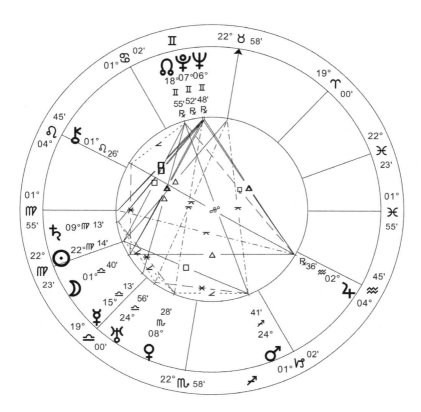

Agatha Christie: 15 September 1890, 04:00 UT
Torquay, England 50°N28' 003°W30'

the prevailing zeitgeist; the spirit of the age. Indeed, the detective genre in which Agatha Christie excelled had its so-called Golden Age in the 1930s, a time when it is agreed she was at the height of her story-telling. That was the era in which Pluto was discovered, the planet of the underworld, and all that it might entail like greed, jealousy, revenge, hatred and murder – familiar themes in her books.

Neptune, the planet of deception and subterfuge, tip-toes down side-streets, presents false information or disappears altogether. In Gemini, Neptune is adept at deception and presenting the red herrings (misleading information) inherent in detective style novels, yet Neptune is also the saviour and that role was given to her investigative protagonists, making all well again.

Neptune also links to music and this was Agatha's first love. Neptune, the god of the Sea, also fostered her love of swimming and surfing. The planet has a connection with poisons too, seemingly her preferred method of despatching people to the next world – in her books of course.

In Gemini, Neptune and Pluto sensitise the nervous system – ruled by Gemini – to a high degree, particularly when channelled through personal planets. The retrograde motion may indicate a strong inner life, the world of imagination and beyond. It certainly advanced her career since the 10th house is involved. The presence of the North Node also indicates a link with the public.

These two High Focus Planets shower luck on creative enterprises through their trine with Jupiter, a Fortune, and through it being in the 5th house, especially since it is the trailing planet: all's well that ends well. In Aquarius Jupiter has the ability to synthesise disparate ideas, and put them into a cohesive whole. The retrograde motion shows inward energy of the mind, rather than performance, as might be otherwise decreed by the 5th house. The emphasis on the Bowl part of the chart in the lower hemisphere containing the personal planets may have added to her inherent shyness, and need for security.

Jupiter, Neptune and Pluto complete a Grand Trine with the Moon, the latter having track with the public. The Moon in Libra indicates justice, and in the 2nd money – often the motive for murder. Aware of the waywardness of money, it was a motivating factor in Agatha's drive towards writing.

Mercury and Uranus also reside in Libra – but in the 3rd house – indicating a quicksilver mind and original thinking. Triumph comes from Mercury's trine to the North Node in 10th and on the Mars/ Jupiter midpoint of success. Mercury gives a hint of structure and longevity by its reception by exaltation with Saturn. Mercury's dearth of aspects promotes an untrammelled mind: she was taught at home, and learnt to think for herself.

Similarly the little grey cells belonging to her Belgian detective Hercule Poirot, reminds us that the element Air dominates, hence reason and logic are used to arrive at conclusions. With mutability taking the edge this shows versatility and adaptability in thinking.

Still in the 3rd house, we have Venus in Scorpio, which in detriment loses its penchant for peace and begins to struggle with the darker side of life. It also rules the 3rd and 10th houses indicating communication and career, and with its sextile to Saturn, leading boundary planet, adds structure. Saturn in Virgo in the 1st may account for the discipline she exerted on her creativity, and also her basic, self-effacing personality. Saturn throws a square to Neptune/Pluto which can cause nervous tension. Was it due to a 'nervous interlude' that she disappeared in 1926?

Of course, the Sun is also in Virgo and it is no surprise perhaps that at a time of need in both world wars she was drawn to pharmaceuticals. Poised on the 2nd house cusp further emphasises her ability to craft her style towards lucrative avenues. The Sun is square Mars in Sagittarius showing her liking for travel and since these two planets make a T-square with the nodes, this shows a basic strength and streak of adventure underneath her shy exterior. Indeed, in an age when middle-class women did not usually work, or travel much, she did both with style.

The Bucket Chart: Two Handle Variation

Description

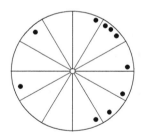

A variation of the Bucket shape is one with two handles but not in conjunction, loosely opposing the main group of planets. Ideally, a distance of around 90° should separate each of the handles from the main group, though 60° minimum separation is often considered.

Energy tends to pour through the two handle planets. If the two planets are in the same house, this suggests one area of life has two separate influences, and expressions.

If there should be a third planet acting as a handle, away from the main group of planets, this begins to have the character of a See-Saw pattern.

Positive traits

There is of course the basic Bowl shape which suggests a sense of containment and protection, but much of the energy of the chart, and of the life, is funnelled through the two handles.

Two handles may suggest two separate strands of energy and life focus, two sides of the personality or two areas of interest, parallel or consecutive. The energies expressed may differ tremendously, or support each other, which of course, depends on the signs, planets, and aspects. There might be a tendency towards duality of character, other things being equal, or two strands of expertise in some direction; probably a complex character.

The person tends to be quite focused within limited parameters, maybe devising their own world, having the ability to make contacts easily though specific to his or her interests.

The faster moving planetary handle should be considered as the High Focus Planet, and chosen first in interpretation: its strength judged by planetary dignity as well as house position.

Like the See-Saw shape, the two-handle Bucket shape may have two spheres of interest but with a difference, at least in a general way. The former prefers to unite with others, whereas the latter prefers to go their own way, or is less ready to compromise.

Challenging Traits

There is not always a forward thrust into any one direction, and there may be some prevarication before a decision is made. The individual may spend time in each area of life at different times. They may cut off one part of their lives, and cut off from certain people, without thought or consideration. Detachment may be a trait that works well in some circumstances, and not so well in others.

It is also possible that if two interests are concurrent, one area may be totally disconnected from the other. This could be almost like two different personalities, which seem to function very well in each area. The focus in two specific areas may make them blind to other aspects of life, and not likely to take advice from anyone not connected to their interests.

Example Bucket Two Handle Variation
Winston Churchill, Statesman and Author

Synopsis

In a 2002 poll, Winston Churchill was voted the Greatest Briton of all time. No mean feat for someone with a chequered political career and worse still, a poor educational history.

His fame rests as the saviour of Britain during WW2, when he led the country to victory against Nazi oppression. It was mainly his strength, determination and oratorical ability which raised the morale of the British people, and those of the colonies.

Although the political arena was his main area of work, he began life as a soldier, revelling in war and proving himself courageous but impetuous. Having been captured during the Boer war, he escaped, wrote about his exploits and became famous.

Biography

Winston Churchill was the son of Lord Randolph Churchill, a brilliant British politician who became leader of the House of Commons and Chancellor of the Exchequer, but died young. His mother was Jennie Jerome, an American socialite. Though born into a privileged background, Winston was not close to his parents during his childhood.

He was a descendant of John Churchill, 1st Duke of Marlborough, 1650-1722, one of England's greatest generals who distinguished himself on the field of battle. Winston wanted to be celebrated like his father and distinguished ancestor, but he showed little promise of the great heights to which he would eventually ascend. He was poor academically, and even though he was to distinguish himself in battle, it took a few attempts to get into the Royal Military College at Sandhurst.

In 1900 he entered the House of Commons, in which he served until 1964. At first he joined the Conservative party, then became a Liberal, and crossed the floor of the House again to the Conservatives. Although an MP he was out of office from 1926 until 1940, often referred to as his wilderness years.

During WW2 he took over from Prime Minister Neville Chamberlain who was not deemed strong enough to lead the country in time of war. Within a few weeks at the helm, he set in motion the evacuation at Dunkirk, code named Operation Dynamo. The rescue of the predominantly British and French armies contributed to saving the Allied Cause.

After he led the British to victory, he was ousted in the 1945 election in favour of the Labour party who promised social change. He was back again as Premier in 1951 until 1956.

Astrology

Triplicities
Fire: Moon, Venus, Sun, Uranus, Neptune
Air: Mars, Jupiter, Saturn
Earth: Pluto
Water: Mercury

Quadruplicities
Cardinal: Mars, Jupiter, Neptune
Fixed: Moon, Mercury, Saturn, Uranus Pluto
Mutable: Sun, Venus

Houses
Angular: Mars
Succedent: Moon, Mercury, Jupiter, Saturn, Uranus, Neptune
Cadent: Venus, Sun, Pluto,

Boundary planets: Saturn/Uranus

Boundary midpoints: 12.25 Scorpio/2nd house

Mutual Reception: Venus/Jupiter

Singleton: Mercury/Water, Pluto/Earth

Churchill is a good example of a two pronged Bucket chart, with Neptune and Pluto as the handles. Outer planets as high focus suggest a global platform. Neptune has the edge in delineation since it is the faster of the two, appropriate in so much as Churchill twice served the navy as the First Lord of the Admiralty: during WW1 (1914-1918) and in 1939 when Britain was involved in WW2, six months before he became Prime Minister.

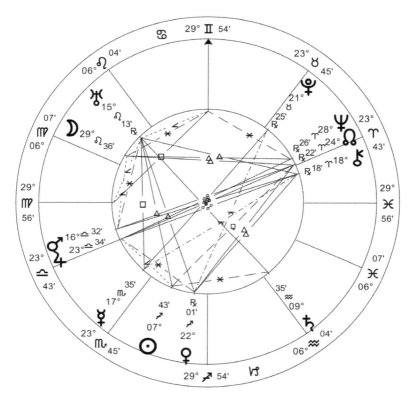

Winston Churchill: 30 November 1874, 01:30
Woodstock, England 51°N52' 001°W21'

In warlike Aries the trident of Neptune becomes a weapon. Churchill saw the gathering war clouds whilst almost everyone else buried their collective head in the sand. Aries is fiercely independent as was Churchill, and perhaps more a soldier than a politician.

As soon as he became Prime Minister in May 1940, he was involved with the amphibious rescue at Dunkirk, and two months later, he was at the inception of the Special Operations Executive (SOE), a subversive and secret underground movement. Both carry the Neptune stamp. The pioneering spirit of Aries slashes through new territory and paves the way for others. In a sense this is what Churchill did when he was at the helm in the war years, clearing the world of debris to provide lands in which men could live freely.

Neptune as the lead handle also represents the saviour, and conjunct the North Node shows a fated life, with alliances made on a wide scale. Chiron in Aries edging towards the 8th house with a close opposition to Mars ruling the 8th house possibly describes the wound of abandonment. There was little contact with his parents. Could this have led to his feeling the wounds of the nation in her time of need?

Jupiter at the other end of the nodal axis in Libra indicates a strong sense of justice, and luck. This is confirmed by a sextile to Venus, the other Fortune, and dallies with her in mutual reception. Placed on the cusp of the 2nd house, money was always plentiful, but paradoxically scarce since there was little limit on extravagance.

Completing Neptune's aspects is the trine to the resplendent Moon in Leo on the elevating fixed star Regulus. Churchill felt he was a man of destiny. Note that both Neptune and the Moon are in sextile to the Midheaven, a signature of ambition, intuition and popularity with the people.

Both handles are placed in the 8th house, the house of struggle and strife, of which he had plenty. Pluto, the other handle in Taurus, spearheads a radical transformation in values and money. In Churchill's early years, the reforms he engineered with Premier Lloyd-George laid the foundation for the welfare state.

His speeches during the war years may have been fashioned from Pluto's opposition to Mercury in Scorpio on the cusp of the 3rd house, which reflects the persuasive and compelling tone of his words in rallying the populace against separatism.[12] Both planets have singleton status furthering their prominence, which is helpful for the ruler of the Ascendant and Midheaven. A Virgo Ascendant teaches us to streamline, organize and economise.[13]

Since the last degree rises on the Virgo Ascendant, this puts much of Libra into the 1st house. Together Virgo and Libra suggest practical application in service and bringing into balance[14] the state of relationship in war and peace, and fairness in the realms of law and justice.

Venus is therefore given weight by ruling Libra, and in Sagittarius in the 3rd house supports Churchill's powers of communication and vision. Its trine with Uranus and North Node, both in Fire, emphasises the inspirational qualities of this element. The 3rd house is further emphasised by the tenancy of the Sun in Sagittarius also with a trine to Uranus, all in all indicating mental virtuosity.

Uranus and Saturn contain the aforementioned planets within their boundary line. Together they combine strength and perseverance[15] summed up in Churchill's attitude of 'we shall never surrender'. The handle planets are always in a relationship with the boundary planets whether in aspect or not. In Churchill's chart this links all three outer planets with Saturn suggesting responsibility of a global scale. Indeed Churchill did carry the world's ills on his shoulders at one of the darkest moments in history.

There are many retrograde planets: constant setbacks and frustration characterised Churchill's political life. He lost more elections than any other political figure in recent British history. His main years of glory rested on those of WW2.

References

1.   *Planetary Patterns*, p.28.
2.   *The Guide to Horoscope Interpretation,* p.77.
3.   ibid
4.   *Combination of Stellar Influences*, p.157.
5.   *Los Angeles Times*, 20 Feb 2017, Archives 4 June 2008, Ann Powers.
6.   Shakespeare, W. *Julius Caesar*, Act 3 Scene 2.
7.   *Encyclopaedia of Medical Astrology*, p.195.
8.   ibid pp.833, 219.
9.   *Esoteric Astrology*, p.143.
10. Al-Biruni. *The Book of Instruction in the Elements of the Art of Astrology,* Ghaznah 1029 AD p.242.
11. *The Combination of Stellar Influences*, p.177.
12. Jansson, Torgny. *Esoteric Astrology, A Beginner's Guide*, Authorhouse, p.116.
13. Lake, Gina. *Symbols of the Soul*, Llewellyn Publications, p.109.
14. *Esoteric Astrology*, pp.145, 265.
15. *The Combination of Stellar Influences*, p.184.

6

The See-Saw Shape and its Variations

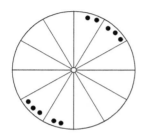

Description

The ideal See-Saw shape has two groups of five planets in relatively close proximity opposite each other in the chart. All the planets in each group should be close but not necessarily in conjunction, and with a reasonably symmetrical formation. The spatial separation on either side of the boundary planets should be no less than 60°[1] though it is usually much more.

The number of planets on each side can, and often does, vary. It may be four planets one side, six the other, the most extreme being three planets one side and seven the other.

Some astrologers class a chart as a See-Saw with two planets on one side and eight on the other. Other astrologers see such a chart as a Bucket shape with two handles.

Life is particularly significant where the planets are concentrated; the affairs of the houses involved are naturally important. Since there are likely to be many opposing aspects, the core opposition – that is between the fastest two planets – is suggested as a good place to begin interpretation.

The boundary planets each side of the See-Saw may have special significance in the chart and life of the individual, as well as their respective midpoints. Planets found on those midpoints usually have an importance in the chart and life.

Like the two-handle Bucket shape, the See-Saw shape may have two spheres of interest. The difference between them – in a general way – is that the former tends to go their own way, whereas the latter has a greater urgency to unite with others or bring the two sides of the nature into a cohesive whole.

Positive Traits

The highest expression of the See-Saw chart may be the search for alignment between the personality and soul. The physical expression could be finding a balance in the psyche or in life's affairs, principally through partnership, personal or business. Integration and understanding of opposite forces may be a life-long search.

Those with this chart shape seek to understand opposing viewpoints, suggesting a good negotiator. The ability to deal with other people contributes to success in life. Such an individual tends to be a good listener, and tries to fulfil other people's wishes. Indeed he or she has a caring, diplomatic quality. Also they are rather good at drawing disparate ideas together, bringing together opposing forces and acting as a mediator.

There may even be two distinct sides to the individual's life, with each group of acquaintances unaware of the other. A clear demarcation between two sets of friends and acquaintances may exist, maybe even living in two different worlds. There may be more than one residence, and they could be a collector, yet the aim is to bring the two sides of the personality into balance.

Challenging Traits

Such individuals may be pulled from one side to the other, and find it very hard to reconcile the two different sides of their lives. When involved in one area, there may be a tug of war with the other.[2] Or whilst giving full attention to one side of their lives, they neglect the other. This might lead to a sense of dissatisfaction, and a feeling of restlessness may result. If there are two extreme sides to the personality, the person may find it hard to compromise, or feels uncomfortable if forced to do so. Difficulty in making up one's mind can occur when subject to two equally opposing viewpoints. Conflicting opportunities sometimes occur in such cases. Duality of character may result.

Associated Planet: The See-Saw chart tries to achieve harmony so the obvious planetary association is Venus, which endeavours to foster a balance in all spheres of activity. (This includes the variations, Hourglass and Butterfly).

Example See-Saw Shape: George Harrison, Musician

Synopsis

George Harrison, sometimes referred to as the quiet Beatle, actually had a lot to say for himself. Were it not so, he would not have written so many wonderful songs, a few becoming classics such as *Here Comes the Sun*, *Something* and *My Sweet Lord*. Reticent and modest he may often have been, yet very much his own person. He was also very forthright and did not suffer fools gladly.

He also has a minor planet named after him, 4149 Harrison, (discovered in 1984) from the middle region of the asteroid belt, roughly between Mars and Jupiter. A variety of the Dahlia flower is named after him too.

Biography

The young George put his heart into music, and didn't like school much, but by the time he was thirty-five he had spent ten years in perhaps the most phenomenally successful band that had ever hit the pop scene, written scores of songs, pioneered the very first charity music festival in 1971 (for Bangladesh) and produced a number of films with HandMade Films. He amassed a great deal of money and helped friends and causes.

He joined Paul McCartney and John Lennon when they were still known as The Quarrymen, a Skiffle group, and played with them in 1960s' Hamburg where he cemented his role within the group. Just a year later, the Beatles were taken over by Brian Epstein under whose guidance they became a tremendous success. 'Beatle Mania' was born. Whilst filming *A Hard Day's Night*, he met his first wife, model Patti Boyd.

Around 1966 Harrison began to take an interest in Eastern religions and Indian music. His influence affected the others in the group who together with their wives, spent some time in India. Meditation and vegetarianism became an important part of George's life. Whilst he tried to live by spiritual principles, he was at the same time drawn to the often wild life of a rock star. He tried to bring the two sides of his life into balance. Certainly he was very generous and helpful to his friends and family, but he also had quite a caustic wit.

Over the years he and his wife Patti became estranged and she left him, subsequently marrying Eric Clapton. In 1979 he married Olivia Arias, a Mexican author and film producer.

In the late 1980s he formed a group called the Traveling Wilburys, which boasted the talents of people like Roy Orbison, Jeff Lynne, Bob Dylan and Tom Petty.

In December 1992 he became the first recipient of the Billboard Century Award, an honour presented to music artists for significant bodies of work. *Rolling Stone* magazine ranked him number 11 in their list of the '100 Greatest Guitarists of All Time'. When he collected the award he was as usual very modest, and said that not much in his life had been planned – it was all a bit haphazard!

In 1999 schizophrenic Beatles fan Michael Abram broke into his home and stabbed George several times, puncturing his lung. George and his wife saw the attack as a spiritual test.

Astrology

Triplicities
Fire: Pluto
Air: Mercury, Saturn, Uranus, Neptune
Earth: Mars
Water: Moon, Venus, Sun, Jupiter

Quadruplicities
Cardinal: Mars, Jupiter, Neptune
Fixed: Moon, Mercury, Pluto
Mutable: Venus, Sun, Saturn, Uranus

Houses
Angular: Sun, Moon, Mercury
Succedent: Venus, Neptune, Saturn, Uranus
Cadent: Mars, Jupiter, Pluto

Reception: Mercury/Saturn

Singleton: Pluto/Fire, Mars/Earth

The chart is a good example of a See-Saw pattern: six planets against four. There were two distinct areas of George's life: the spiritual and the material, almost competing for supremacy.

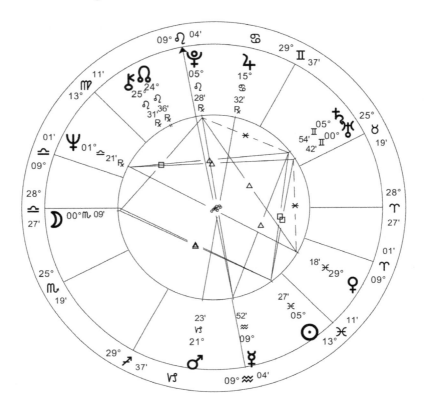

George Harrison: 24 February 1943, 23:42 BST
Liverpool, England 53°N25' 002°W55'

The core opposition is between Mars and Jupiter, both exalted, therefore signifying at the start that success in life is likely. The core opposition in cadent houses is like activity behind the scenes. There are two further exaltations: Venus in Pisces, and Mercury in Aquarius, from a modernistic viewpoint, indicating blessings from the gods. The little Fire in the chart creates a persona that does not put all their wares in the shop window.

The exalted Mars, further strengthened by its singleton status, is the High Focus Planet. In Capricorn it gives the potential to rise to the top, both materially and spiritually. Exalted Jupiter in Cancer can create a mass following. Across the 3rd/9th houses we see excellent communication abilities with the possibility of searching for the divine in man, the 9th being the house of God.

George said, "Everything else can wait, but the search for God cannot."[3]

Mars is semi-square the Sun, and sesquiquadrate Saturn, in the 8th house of shared resources. When these three planets are brought together in an aspectual relationship there is often intense self-awareness about the meaning of life through tests and trials. Opportunity to understand comes through Saturn's lessons.[4] One test was the law suit for plagiarism regarding *My Sweet Lord*. The law suit went on for years, and even when George was willing to give the song and the money away, the other side wouldn't let it rest.

The Sun in Pisces represents both the limitation and liberation of matter. In the 4th house this is linked to the land indicating the struggle he had in fulfilling his need for spirituality and coming to terms with earthly matters. He did feel most at peace when he spent time in his large garden. Many people found some refuge living in his home. The Sun trine Moon on Ascendant emphasises his link with the masses.

All-important exalted Venus, ruler of the Ascendant, is in Pisces too, but in the 5th house, indicating his success with creative pursuits. Indeed Venus has her Joy in the 5th, and associated with the See-Saw shape, it shows harmony and friendship through performance.

That he was attracted to the mystical and brought it into his music and songwriting is reflected in the opposition of Venus to Neptune. In fact Venus is also sextile Uranus and trine Pluto, thus aspecting all the outer planets and it is no wonder George actually wanted to see God, as the lyrics to *My Sweet Lord* testify.

Pluto of course dominates the chart from the Midheaven, and there is no doubt that George, once unshackled from the rock group, slipped gently yet powerfully into his own personal style. He had a very profound effect on the world through his songs. Pluto's singleton status in Fire strengthens its magnetic quality. Pluto draws in the square from the Moon in Scorpio on the Ascendant. This brings a tremendous connection with the public, with a rather deep and reserved style. But George was nobody's fool.

Pluto gives persuasive powers and razor-sharp wit through an opposition to Mercury, planet of communication. Mercury has a very serious side since it is trine Saturn, as well as in mutual reception.

Saturn and Uranus in Gemini in the 8th house hint at transformation on a deep level.

In 1966, still only 23 years of age, George realised that despite enjoying the trappings of fame, material success could not satisfy some inner yearning. He turned towards Eastern religions in his search for enlightenment, in a deep and wholehearted way and a struggle ensued between the material and spiritual life.

Libra on the Ascendant is concerned with balance as is indeed the See-Saw chart: both rule the concept of choice. In George's case the choices were on a much larger scale than individuals who don't have such fame and wealth. At first he went to extremes, becoming a strict vegetarian, meditating for hours at a time, and becoming more remote. At the same time he indulged in alcohol, took drugs and had lots of affairs which contributed to the break-up with his first wife Patti Boyd. He fought hard to reconcile the opposing sides of his nature.

Example See-Saw Shape: Kim Philby, Spy

Synopsis
Kim Philby was part of the Cambridge Five spy ring which hooked itself into the public consciousness in 1951. It was the defection of Guy Burgess and Donald Maclean to Moscow that exposed him and eventually the other two: Anthony Blunt and John Cairncross.

It was the worst case of espionage and betrayal ever to have occurred in the United Kingdom.

In the 1920s and 1930s Europe was threatened by Fascism (Hitler and Mussolini) and at the time, Communism, waving the banner of equality, appeared to be the only bulwark against Fascism's restrictive ideology. These young students at Cambridge University seemingly driven by a sense of idealism were in time to betray their country for their beliefs.

Biography
Philby was born Harold Adrian Russell Philby in Amballa, India, nicknamed 'Kim' after the book of the same name by author Rudyard Kipling. His father – Harry St John Philby – was a member of the Indian Civil Service.

Philby spent most of his life profiting from the capitalistic system that he despised. He enjoyed a first class education at public school, worked in top jobs in journalism and intelligence, and his children benefited from private schooling. Money flowed through his fingers like the copious amounts of alcohol which flowed through his gullet.

In 1937 Philby reported on the Spanish Civil War for *The Times* from the Nationalist viewpoint. The future fascist dictator General Francisco Franco, in gratitude for Philby's pro-fascist articles, awarded him the Red Cross of Military Merit in 1938. All the time Philby had been sending back information about the Nationalists' movements to both his British and Soviet (Communist) masters.

In 1940 Philby was recruited by the British Secret Intelligence Service (SIS) to head its anti-Soviet Branch! Philby, in the right place for spiriting away sensitive material, must have thanked his lucky stars. Once WW2 ended, Philby received the Order of the British Empire for his war-time work – and continued to send classified information to the Soviets, who were no longer allies.

Secrets are the currency of the intelligence world, and friendship the means by which one spends it. Agents lead a double-life, unable to discuss their work with family and friends, so they discuss it with colleagues instead. One department becomes aware of what the other is doing.

In 1951, the Venona project, a counter-intelligence program initiated by the United States Army to decrypt messages sent by Soviet Union intelligence agencies, revealed the names of possible spies, among them Donald MacLean. Philby warned his friend, who subsequently defected to the Soviet Union along with Guy Burgess. In doing so, Philby spread a cloak of suspicion upon his own guilt.

Suspicion was not hard evidence and Philby was not charged. Nevertheless he lost his lucrative position in the intelligence service. A few years later, with powerful friends lobbying on his behalf, Philby was reinstated as a secret agent. His field of operation was Beirut.

In 1963 – just as British intelligence was closing in on him, he defected to the Soviet Union. In Moscow, Philby was showered with medals, but no job of importance. He wasn't totally trusted by his new country. The irony was that the country that he had been steadily betraying had trusted him completely.

Astrology

Triplicities
Fire: Mercury, Jupiter
Air: Pluto
Earth: Moon, Sun, Mars, Saturn, Uranus
Water: Venus, Neptune

Quadruplicities
Cardinal: Sun, Uranus, Neptune
Fixed: Moon, Mars, Venus, Saturn
Mutable: Mercury, Jupiter, Pluto

Houses
Angular: Moon, Venus
Succedent: Mercury, Sun, Pluto
Cadent: Moon, Mars, Saturn, Uranus, Neptune

Reception: Venus/Mars

Singleton: Pluto (Air)

There is a perfect balance of 5 planets either side of the MC/IC line which constitutes the ideal See-Saw chart. There was a clear demarcation between the two areas of Philby's life; he was in effect a double agent.

Kim Philby said, "I am really two people. I am a private person and a political person. Of course if there is a conflict, the political person comes first."[5]

The core opposition which begins interpretation is the one between the Moon and Venus across the horizon. The Moon, the High Focus Planet, is strong by exaltation in Taurus which inclines to a desire for the good life[6], and was readily fulfilled! Taurus on the Ascendant concurs with this but also endeavours to establish a sense of values.

There may be ambivalence where the material world is concerned since the Moon straddles both the 1st and 12th houses emphasising the self and the not-self. Venus, Ascendant ruler in its detriment in Scorpio, loses its equanimity and is now aroused to conflict, wrestling with finances and power. This is easily affected since she slides into reception with Mars.

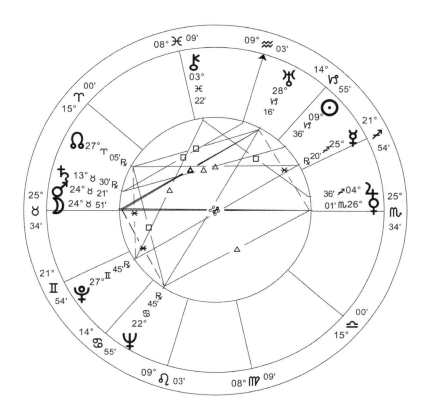

Kim Philby: 1 January 1912, 14:30 IST -5:30
Ambala, India 30°N21' 076°E50'

The interplay between the Moon, Venus and Mars across the horizon accounts for the dazzling charm Philby used to beguile others. The Moon and Ascendant on the Venus/Mars midpoint underscores his attractive personality. No one believed he could ever be a spy!

The Moon's rulership of the 3rd house and sextile to Neptune therein, shows an intuitive grasp of prevailing trends. Good luck followed Philby in and out of scrapes, aided and abetted by the strong Jupiter in domicile conjunct Venus. With two benefics in the 7th house even his enemies liked him! The strong Jupiter ruling the 11th house shows that his friends stayed true even after his spying was rumbled.

Beneath the bonhomie lurked the spectre of the 12th house. It is a house that embraces universal consciousness and unity with others reflecting the communistic ideology of everyone being the same. Mars in Taurus, its detriment, struggles with materialism against universal ideals, whilst Saturn strives to rebuild the world with a new edifice. Saturn in the 12th, ruling the MC, the career, is an excellent signature for undercover work.

Psychologically, the 12th house has a tenuous link to terrestrial life, and in some cases, gives a sense of isolation and separation. Philby did not see himself as a traitor to his country. He said, "To betray, you must first belong, I never belonged".[7]

Saturn is semi-square Pluto in Gemini 2nd house, where there is a suggestion of values being overturned or holding two conflicting sets of values. The singleton status of Pluto confers greater prominence in matters of money: he had it all, and then he lost it helping a friend to defect to Russia. But he got it all back again since Pluto opposes Mercury in the 8th showing persuasive ability in speaking and writing. He was also asked to do this in his position in Beirut – that is, spy on others under the guise of journalism.

Also in the 8th is the Sun in Capricorn, which can reach the heights of personal ambition or the heights of spiritual consciousness, so a struggle ensues. In Capricorn decisions can be made without bias or emotion for the greater good, or for the self. To be a spy one has to have a cool head since it is a dual life where even the nearest and dearest are not usually cognisant of what lies beneath. With the Sun in the 8th, a secret way of life comes naturally especially with the trine to Saturn in the 12th. The Sun's sesquiquadrate to Mars in the 12th creates the soldier of God, the crusader, perhaps giving a sense of omniscience; saving the world. Ideals drove Philby to act as a spy, he maintained, not money, but that came his way anyway, with lucrative work from the country he betrayed.

In the 12th house, however, there exists something of a conundrum. The North Node placed therein is in Aries; the first sign in the last house. There is a push for the collective good – giving a saviour mentality – but perhaps as long as one can be the leader. One of Philby's favourite songs was *My Way*!

The nodes uphold his idealistic notions since they link in Grand Cross formation with Uranus and Neptune, the outer planets standing for the collective and/or global consciousness. Across the 3/9th houses, it would seem that he looked far to fulfil his idealistic dreams.

The See-Saw Chart: Hourglass Variation

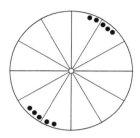

Description

The Hourglass shape is a much tighter variation of the See-Saw, and does not seem to appear with great frequency. An equal number of planets either side is of course the ideal but an Hourglass, like the See-Saw, can vary in planetary quantity on either side of the chart. Three planets against nine could still reflect an Hourglass shape depending on closeness of planets either side.

Some astrologers might suggest that as little as two on one side and eight on the other[8] would still be classified as an Hourglass but such a combination would lose the symmetrical form which underlies the Hourglass (and See-Saw) shape. The shape Jones calls a See-Saw, Jansky calls an Hourglass. Since the Hourglass is a tighter version of the See-Saw, it might follow that there is greater focus on aims or working within tighter parameters, for good or ill.

The minimum open space on either side of the central axis should at least be 90° between boundary planets.

The chart will be dominated by oppositions, and the pure Hourglass is unlikely to have different types of traditional aspects, except to the Ascendant and Midheaven, although there may be some inconjuncts, semi-squares and sesquiquadrates.

The core opposition will be pivotal to interpretation – determined by the faster moving planets. This provides the driving force.[9]

Boundary planets on either side of the space between the two groups may also be highlighted together with their aspects and midpoints. Check to see if a planet falls in aspect to the midpoints made by these planets.

Positive Traits

Like a spear thrown in a one-pointed direction, so does life often follow a definite course with such a chart. Concerted effort is expended in a particular area of life or two particular areas. There is an ability to see both sides of the equation, and gauge the opposition.

The search for harmony endeavours to bring the two sides of the nature into balance, but just as easily the balance can be tipped over. Then the search for balance starts all over again in whichever area of life this is expressed.

A far-seeing quality may give a sense of good timing. A good strategist, able to work out the moves of others in the theatre of play, or war. Contemplative on one hand, but a good combatant on the other. There is often the ability to hold two views at once, going from one to the other. Or indeed, there may be an escape from one area of life to the other.

There could be many choices in life, often with extremes, before a compromise is sought. The person can be a bridge-builder and able to link different ideas together to make a whole.

Challenging Traits

Due to a tight hold on energy these people can be quite highly strung, and may over-react to situations. This could result in aloofness, but largely due to sensitivity to circumstances, and they may retire if hurt.

Fortunes can be extreme in either direction, and may polarise opinion, sometimes popular and successful, sometimes not so much. When involved in one area of life, they may ignore the other area and maybe the people in it. Or circumstances decree that this happens.

Associated Planet: Venus

Example Hourglass Shape: Noel Coward, Entertainer

Synopsis

Called The Master by many, Noel Coward's theatrical work continues to influence the entertainment industry. He excelled as a playwright, composer, director, actor and comedian as well as artist. He stood out for his personal style which combined flamboyance with sophistication.

Though he was born into a middle-class background, he gave the impression of coming from high society, and indeed it is that milieu in which his plays were set. His titles include *Hayfever*, *Private Lives*, *Present Laughter* and *Blithe Spirit*. One of his most famous films/plays was *Brief Encounter* which tells of a forbidden love: homosexuality. Still illegal when it written, Coward had to make the forbidden love one of infidelity in a heterosexual marriage.

Biography

Coward was extremely versatile within the theatrical scene. For someone who couldn't read or write music, he put together hundreds of songs – words and music. He knew his limitations against other greats in the theatre in terms of acting, voice and looks, but he always felt he could score by his charisma and magnetism.

In the theatre since age eleven, his stagecraft was outstanding. Of the many ladies he starred with in the theatre his favourite was Gertrude Lawrence, who he felt had instinctive acting ability and timing. He reached into the highest echelons of celebrity, being on good terms with the Queen's uncle, Lord Mountbatten, and the Duke of Kent.

His life took a different turn during WW2. He worked for the British Secret Service, and ran the British propaganda office in Paris. He was vilified in the press during the war for his travels, supposedly for pleasure, but in reality he was working for Intelligence. (It has since been learnt that he had been on Hitler's death list since Coward opposed appeasement and was an armed forces entertainer mocking Hitler).

Further popularity was lost when he did in fact leave England as a tax exile. Nevertheless, his plays continued to be successful and he remained a star until the very end, although his popularity took a dip during the rise of the 'kitchen-sink dramas' in late 1950s and early 60s. A revival of his plays a few years later put him back in the spotlight.

After a string of successes in London and Broadway, he took up the cudgels of parenthood – looking after orphans. He became president of the Actors Orphanage, where children of actors were placed whose parents for one reason or another could not look after them. He remained in this post for twenty-two years and brought many useful changes to the establishment.

A theatre in London is named after him: the Noel Coward Theatre. He was knighted in 1969.

Astrology

Triplicities
Fire: Mercury, Sun, Saturn, Uranus
Air: Moon, Neptune, Pluto
Earth: Venus, Mars
Water: Jupiter

Quadruplicities
Cardinal: Venus, Mars
Fixed: Jupiter
Mutable: Moon, Mercury, Sun, Saturn, Uranus, Neptune, Pluto

Houses
Angular: None
Succedent: Moon, Mercury, Jupiter, Uranus, Pluto
Cadent: Sun, Venus, Mars, Saturn, Neptune

Reception: None

Singletons: Jupiter – Water and Fixed – twice

The intense focus of the Hourglass shape figured early in Coward's life, since his vocation was never in doubt. Oppositions abound in an Hourglass shape, which can often polarize opinion. Indeed, Coward's play *Sirocco* in the early 1920s brought harsh criticism; he offended theatre goers by dealing with the subject of free love.

The core opposition involves the traditional planets Moon/Mercury across Gemini/Sagittarius, creating mental flexibility and versatility. The Moon, the High Focus Planet in 9th house puts emphasis on the higher mind, and ruling the 10th house indicates fame/career to be the spur. It is semi-square the Midheaven with a link to the nodes, assuring a doting public. Luna is in conjunction with Pluto and opposition Uranus, giving depth and originality.

It was his gift with words that pulled Coward out of the common mould (he saw himself predominantly as a writer), helped by having Pluto on what is known as the 'writer's degree', 15 Gemini.[10] And since Pluto and its semi-square to the MC are on the midpoint of success Mars/Jupiter, phenomenal it was.

The interesting connection is Chiron opposing Pluto. Could it have

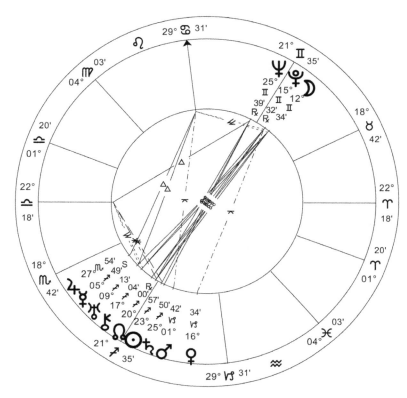

Noel Coward: 16 December 1899, 2:30 UT
Teddington, England 51°N26' 000°W20'

been his secret homosexuality, which dared not voice its name? Secrets also abound with Pluto in undercover work and its prominence could reflect Coward's spell in Intelligence during WW2.

Though his plays have an ostensibly light, comedic touch, many dealt with taboo subjects such as drug abuse and sexual vanity, for instance in *The Vortex*. Some critics saw the latter as a metaphor for homosexuality. This play brought him fame and money. Pluto on cusp of 8th/9th cusp breaks down boundaries, and looks for greater freedom of expression.

The outer planets indicate a more global connection, but also pull on the nerves in Gemini. Indeed, Coward drove himself hard and collapsed in 1926. Mutability dominates the chart which shows versatility and restlessness of mind and body. Certainly Coward's mind was constantly on alert and he travelled a great deal.

Mercury at the other end of the core opposition is in detriment in Sagittarius helping to focus ideas. There was always a message in Coward's plays and songs. Mercury rules 9th house of higher mind and universal connections and the 11th house of groups – Coward had a genius for friendship. Mercury is conjunct Jupiter adding to the intellect and a favourable trine to the Midheaven boosts the career. With Jupiter ruling the 5th house, and its singleton position, this heralds excellence in stagecraft.

Sagittarius is strongly emphasised with the Sun therein promising far-sightedness, and the appetite for life that is taken seriously due to the conjunction to Mars and Saturn. Such a combination often shows up in lives where self-awareness is deepened through obstacles and challenges. Coward's capacity for hard work reflects this conjunction, not only in his normal theatre work but also the extraordinary number of concerts he gave to the wounded in hospitals during the war.

The Sun's opposition to Neptune suggests interest in spiritual matters, or certainly a strong imagination. One of his more successful plays was *Blithe Spirit*, a comedy involving the occult. In the 3rd house these planets underscore his quicksilver mind.

Capricorn is represented in the 3rd house as well, with the tenancy of the exalted Mars which rules 2nd, 6th and 7th indicating the money that flowed in through hard work and ease of contact. Venus is here too, and in Capricorn signifies reaching for the heights in material or spiritual ambition. Venus is linked to the See-Saw/Hourglass type of chart, and governs the sense of unity through love and understanding, but it has a dearth of aspects and since it rules the Ascendant, it is possible that Coward held himself a little apart from his fellow men. He was convivial and gregarious in play, but rather private in personal life.

Noel Coward was knighted by Her Majesty the Queen in her New Year's Honours List in 1971.

The See-Saw Chart Shape: Butterfly Variety

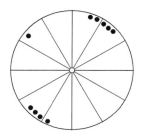

Description

A variation of the See-Saw, the Butterfly shape, has one planet roughly equidistant from two aggregations of planets on either side of the chart, in whichever quarter or hemisphere, or cutting across them. There should be a semblance of symmetry in the two groups of planets – like butterfly wings! The empty space on either side of the two groups should ideally be at least 90°. The energy of the two opposing sides is channelled through the single planet, the High Focus Planet.

There is often a T-square formed between the single planet and one or two of the planets on opposing sides.

If there are two planets in conjunction equidistant from the two planetary groups, this may signify a Splay or Tripod shape especially if there is a lack of symmetry.

Boundary planets on either side may well be significant. The one where the lone planet crosses the nearest Boundary line may be of greater importance, almost acting like a midpoint. This actually may form a midpoint, and the house where the midpoint falls is usually of importance.

Positive Traits

This shape often gives referee tactics, with the ability to intervene, or even pacify two opposing factions. How the individual approaches such a situation depends upon the state of the single planet, its modus operandi and its strength in terms of its dignities, sign, house and aspects.

Life may be lived in finding that balance and centre within themselves, though usually through relationships with others.

It is possible that circumstances early in life put the individual in a position where he or she had to play one faction off against the other, as in tricky domestic circumstances. The result is an uncanny ability to see both sides of any situation and then amalgamate the differences.

This could reveal someone who learns survival tactics early in life which stand them in good stead later on. This then becomes their strength. Certainly there is an ability to manoeuvre around difficult circumstances. A good strategist.

Challenging Traits

Much energy goes into the planet standing at the apex of the two distinct planetary groups, which can be a tower of strength or bring challenge and struggle, hopefully leading to wisdom and eventual power. Stressful circumstances may arise where the individual has to cope alone, or depend upon himself.

At certain times conditions can be overwhelming leading to withdrawal from life, which is probably the best course of action otherwise there may be a threat of breakdown. It very much depends upon the strength of the single planet just how likely this is to happen.

There may be the possibility of being all things to all men, going along with other people's ideas just to keep the peace. Too much of this and there could be a loss of autonomy, with a resulting loss of identity. Or that's how it may feel.

Associated Planet: Venus

Example Butterfly Shape: Lord George Gordon Noel Byron, Poet

Synopsis

Lord Byron is one of England's greatest poets, and a leading figure in the Romantic Movement (late 18th/early 19th century) characterised by its emphasis on emotion and individualism. Byron first reached the heights of success with his poem *Childe Harold's Pilgrimage*, written after his Grand Tour of Europe, something usually undertaken by aristocratic young men, or those of means.

Unfortunately, the young Lord never did have much means. He inherited the title from his uncle, but not much money to go with it.

Lady Caroline Lamb termed him mad, bad and dangerous to know, and the quote lives on in infamy.

Biography

Byron's mother was emotionally erratic, loving one moment, aloof the next, and his father absent. Like so many others, Lady Caroline Lamb fell for the good-looking young Lord, but it was not to last. Indeed, she was already married to Lord Melbourne, a future Prime Minister of England.

Byron's one true love, so it seems, was his half-sister Augusta Leigh, though the lady was married. Although the relationship was technically incestuous, they did not meet until their teens so they were new acquaintances, as it were. She was the only one who could tame the unruly Lord. Money worries, the scandal of his relationship with Augusta, and rather indiscreet words spoken about the Prince Regent forced him abroad where seven years later he died.

There was one marriage just before he left, to Annabella Milbanke, which was disastrous largely because he married her for her money, and she in an effort to tame him. A child resulting from this union was the future Ada Lovelace (who contributed to the founding of computer science). Byron had an enormous capacity for friendship; people truly loved him, except his former wife, but that is quite understandable since he treated her abominably.

In his travels across Europe accompanied by his pet bear he met up with fellow poet Percy Bysshe Shelley, and his wife Mary Shelley. One evening they dared each other to write a ghost story, and that is how Mary came to write the novel *Frankenstein*.

Byron lived a rather dissolute life, excessive in almost every way, reputedly having affairs with both men and women, as well as indulging in the odd orgy or two. It is possible that he suffered from syphilis (as many people did in those days since there was no real cure). It seems that his early death might have been his own self-undoing since he went out in a storm, didn't bother to dry off, and caught a fever. But whether it was the fever that killed him or the tender ministrations of his various doctors cannot at this distance of time be judged.

Byron is greatly honoured in Greece.

Astrology

Triplicities
Fire: none
Air: Venus, Sun, Jupiter, Saturn, Neptune, Pluto
Earth: Mercury
Water: Moon, Mars, Uranus

Quadruplicities
Cardinal: Moon, Mercury, Mars, Uranus, Neptune
Fixed: Venus, Sun, Saturn, Pluto
Mutable: Jupiter

Houses
Angular: Mercury, Mars, Saturn
Succedent: Moon, Sun, Uranus, Neptune
Cadent: Venus, Jupiter, Pluto

Reception: None

Singleton: Jupiter (Mutable), Mercury (Earth)

Two planetary groups span either side of the chart, linked by the single planet at the bottom, quite typical of a Butterfly shape. The young Byron soon learnt how to pitch against conflicting sides when he witnessed his mother's tirade against a dissolute husband. His mother's moods were unpredictable: loving one moment, aloof the next. Although this too characterised Byron's own behaviour, it did not stop him attracting a great many people into his life, true to this shape as well.

These contrasting feelings found themselves centred on a relationship with his half-sister Augusta, who gave him the love and understanding that he craved, but who could never be his, even if she were not already married, since it was an incestuous union.

The lynchpin to these two sides of his nature was Neptune in Libra in the 5th house, which has little to recommend it for stability but is highly endorsed for compassion, vision and creativity. Libra strives for balance, but Neptune does not provide a structured framework upon which to achieve it. In the wake of failed love affairs, he poured his feelings into poetry.

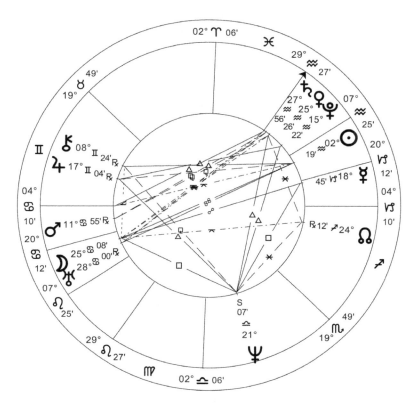

Lord Byron: 22 January 1788 NT, 14:00 LMT
London, England 51°N30' 000°W10'

The hero in his epic poem *Childe Harold's Pilgrimage* seeks a perfection that he cannot attain. Ultimately the hero of the poem becomes an outcast. This turned out to be somewhat autobiographical. Neptune is in a T-Square with the Moon, Mercury and Uranus, which indicates quick thinking and a highly active nervous system, underscored by the midpoints these planets make with each other.[11] The Moon rules the Ascendant and with its conjunction to Uranus shows originality and unpredictability. Uranus opposes the Sun, so greatly influences the Lights, giving a touch of genius and volatility.

The release of feeling into poetry comes from Neptune's Grand Trine with the two Fortunes, Venus and Jupiter. Venus is not far from the Midheaven though it has to get over Saturn to reach there.

Its conjunction to the cold planet and in Aquarius shows the rather detached side of Byron. Saturn, a boundary planet, is on 10th house cusp and traditionally heralds a downfall[12] which occurred in 1816 around his Saturn return, when his reputation was tarnished by scandal.

The planetary wings of the Butterfly shape put the emphasis on Cancer and Aquarius, which reflects Byron's paradoxical needs for closeness and freedom. The Sun in Aquarius, in detriment, takes the emphasis off the self and entertains the idea of the group. This was expressed by Byron's conquest of society in a milieu where he received 'pop-star' adulation. Unity of brotherhood are the higher qualities of the group[13] which Byron too expressed.

Neptune is linked to the boundary planets at the top and bottom of the chart by midpoint. These are Mercury/Uranus and Jupiter/Saturn which suggest tremendous inspiration and vision, nerve trouble, as well as emotional tensions and changing fortunes.[14]

Jupiter, a boundary planet, is given emphasis since it is the only planet in mutable signs. In Gemini, and in detriment, the duality of this sign can lead to versatility as well as instability. In the 12th house Jupiter is motivated by high ideals and strives towards an inner union with God, since this is one of the occult houses.[15] Byron's metaphysical poem *Manfred* shows an individual tortured by guilt who hopes to escape the torment by summoning spirits to help him:

> I should be sole in this sweet solitude,
> And with the spirit of the place divide
> The homage of these waters

The chart is heavy on Air and cardinal planets, which brings the focus back to Libra – cardinal Air – and the need for balance and the perfection of the human spirit, reflected in Neptune. Not always attainable on the material level. However, some of Byron's poetry is truly sublime.

At the time of his death in the Greek town of Missolonghi – 19th April 1824 at 6:00pm – Byron had taken up the cause for Greek independence (from the Ottoman Empire), in true Aquarian style. But before he could fire a shot he was dead. There is a possibility pneumonia (inflammatory condition of lungs) killed him. There is no Fire in the chart which may suggest a sluggish, cold organism.

References
1. *The Guide to Horoscope Interpretation*, p.90.
2. ibid p.91.
3. www.brainyquotes.com
4. *Esoteric Astrology*, p.284.
5. 'The Spy Who Loved Me: Charlotte Philby', *The Independent*, (6 March 2010 www.independent.co.uk)
6. Jansson, Torgny. *Esoteric Astrology, A Beginner's Guide*, Authorhouse, 2005, p.36.
7. *Sunday Times*, London 17 Dec 1967
8. *Planetary Patterns*, p.29.
9. ibid p.31.
10. Carter, Charles. *An Encyclopaedia of Psychological Astrology*. Theosophical Publishing House, 1924/1963, p.118.
11. *The Combination of Stellar Influences*, pp 125, 197.
12. Lilly, Wm. *Christian Astrology*, Regulus, 1647, 1985, p.620.
13. Weiner, Errol. *Transpersonal Astrology*, Element, p.182.
14. *The Combination of Stellar Influences*, pp.124,170.
15. *The Encyclopaedia of Medical Astrology*, p.881.

7

The Splay Shape and its Variation

Description

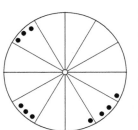

The Splay shape often appears a little haphazard, as if having no shape at all. However, ideally it has three clusters of planets, usually at irregular intervals[1] with at least a minimum 60° arc of separation.

Variations can include four or five aggregations of planets which will of course lessen the degrees of arc between each cluster, but that may be the only shape obvious in the chart.

The ideal Splay has almost the same number in each cluster, but that is rare. The minimum in each cluster of planets should be two. One planet standing alone makes the shape a Tripod – a variation of Splay.

The Splay shape tends to contain a Grand Trine, T-Square or a Grand Cross, or all three. The latter two aspect patterns create a more dynamic centre to the personality.

The core opposition between the two fastest moving planets may be the place to start analysis, and could well be the backbone to the chart. The faster moving planet is the High Focus Planet. This has also been called the reins planet – leading the others.[2] But if there is a Grand Trine instead of oppositions in the chart, then the HFP is the fastest mover in this configuration.

Positive Traits

There is an inner assurance, and striving to be true to what he or she feels inside; these people are not usually bothered by what others think. Purposeful in intent and once convinced in any direction, the Splay individual is not easily thwarted in design. This makes them rather unpredictable and not easily defined, since they go their own way in life. There is an aversion to conformity, eschewing tradition, often moving in an opposite direction to expectation. They are rather difficult to pigeon-hole.

The individual moves easily from different areas of commitment or interest in their life, which are usually distinct from each other. This may give them an air of mystery, though that is not necessarily deliberate.

A keen observer, with a profound knowledge of various subjects often leads to good strategic or psychological acumen. They can be inventive and pioneering, introducing a new line of thought in different areas of life, such as writing, art, science etc. The certainty of their cause can give them a strong personality, and a need for free expression. There could be excellent ability or talent in these different areas.

Challenging Traits

Once such individuals get an idea into their head, they can be quite intense and resist compromise which can bring many storms into the life, but they know how to pitch one group of people against another. Though they play their cards close to their chest, they usually speak out on what they truly believe.

Such strong individuality makes them difficult to understand at times. They don't easily adapt to others, which does not always make for smooth relations. Often people have to adapt to them, not that the Splay type necessarily seek that consciously, but they aren't too bothered about what others might think. There may be a struggle to find the right niche in life since they can be something of an outsider, and do not always fit easily into society.

Quite possibly they do not object to being alone as then they can follow their own routine.

Associated Planet

The Splay shape with its penchant for individualism might accord well with the Sun's drive towards holism. The Sun is the centre of the self and draws together disparate ideas. The individuality of the Splay chart, being true to itself, strives for autonomy like the Sun. (This includes the variation Tripod).

Example Splay Shape: Annie Besant, Theosophist

Synopsis

Annie Besant, the 2nd President of the Theosophical Society since its inception, insisted on living her own truth. The price for following such an individualistic life path was high. Marriage to a clergyman brought disillusionment with Christianity and she left her marriage, and lost her children.

A subsequent life as a political activist on behalf of the disadvantaged saw her involved in many worthy causes. She finally found what may have been the heart of her search; a belief in the ancient wisdom espoused by theosophy.

Theosophy seeks the nature of divinity and the truth which links all religions and which offers a path towards knowledge and enlightenment.

Biography

Annie was born into a Christian family and since girlhood she wanted to devote her life to God. Instead she married a clergyman and lived to regret it. She found her husband controlling and even violent. Annie couldn't toe the line as a vicar's wife – refusing to go to church obviously did not put him in the best of moods.

In following her own path, and searching for a new belief and truth, she knew she would have to make sacrifices. She knew she hurt her mother by disowning Christianity, and that she would lose her husband and children if she renounced her marriage – Victorian morality was quite strict on that score. To leave a husband was not only scandalous, it made her an outcast and put her on the breadline.

She embarked on a life fighting injustice wherever she found it. This included the Rights of Women, Child Labour, and supporting the Match Girl Strike of 1888 (which brought them better conditions). She also supported Irish Home Rule. These were not popular issues with the establishment.

Then in 1889 she met Helena Blavatsky and discovered theosophy and her interest in secular matters waned. After she read *The Secret Doctrine* her life changed. She became a theosophist and in 1894 moved to India, looking for inner meaning.

With her excellent oratorical ability, Annie had an amazing effect on people. Whilst in India she championed Indian Home Rule. It seems she needed a cause, and to fight injustice wherever she witnessed it.

She travelled to the United States with her protégé and adopted son Jiddu Krishnamurti who she claimed was the new Messiah and incarnation of Buddha. They formed a very close bond for a number of years, but eventually, in 1929, Krishnamurti rejected claims of divinity. Annie continued to campaign for Indian independence and for the causes of theosophy until her death in 1933.

Astrology

Triplicities
Fire: Uranus, Pluto
Air: Mercury, Venus, Sun, Neptune
Earth: Mars
Water: Moon, Jupiter, Saturn

Quadruplicities
Cardinal: Moon, Mercury, Venus, Sun, Jupiter, Uranus, Pluto,
Fixed: Mars, Neptune
Mutable: Saturn

Houses
Angular: Moon, Mercury, Venus, Sun, Mars, Jupiter, Uranus, Pluto
Succedent: None
Cadent: Saturn, Neptune

Reception: Saturn/Neptune

Singletons: Mars (Earth), Saturn (Mutable)

There are four well defined planetary clusters suggestive of a Splay shape. With its inclusion of oppositions and a T-square, this creates a challenging, dynamic nature. Such individualism has no truck with compromise, or hypocrisy. Such was Annie Besant.

The core opposition Mercury/Uranus immediately suggests an original, dynamic thinker and speaker, qualities which reflect the independent, unconventional behaviour of the Splay chart. Mercury in Libra acts as the mediator between opposing factions striving for

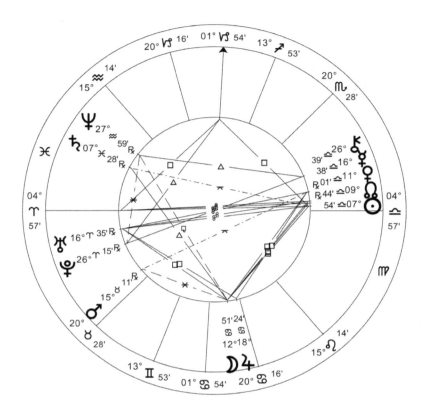

Annie Besant: 1 October 1847, 17:29 LMT
London, England 51°N30' 000°W10'

eventual harmony and justice. Uranus in Aries shows the trailblazer
and a need for autonomous action. Across the 1st/7th house axis of
alliances, right relations between people were her goal. The midpoints
linked to Mercury and Uranus – Sun/Pluto and Moon/Jupiter –
indicate success in oratory.[3]

Uranus opposing the planets in Libra further suggests a basic nonconformist quality, as well as humanitarian principles. The Sun in Libra
fights for justice. Associated with the Splay shape, the Sun indicates
Annie's initiative towards wholeness lay in diverting attention from the
self and highlighting the plight of others. She spoke publicly about
birth control, which at the time was illegal, and also questioned the
status of the Church of England, advocating a secular state.

The North Node conjunct the Sun and other planets in Libra creates a strong link with the public in many areas. Venus in domicile endeavours to effect a balance between self and others. The conjunction to Mercury gives an ability to mediate between two factions as indeed between the Match Girls and the Employers.

Chiron in the 7th may illustrate the wounds of others which spurred her into doing battle with authority/establishment. Chiron trine Neptune in the 12th indicates compassion for the world's ills, but this also breeds adversaries since the 7th and 12th houses are linked with enemies: a nonconformist like Annie usually has a few of those. In her case, those who stood for traditional authority.

Neptune and Saturn in the 12th house and mutual reception tear at the boundaries of the material world. Here there is a feeling of being one with all, a saviour mentality. Saturn and Neptune aspect the strong Moon and Jupiter – in domicile and exaltation respectively – by trine and sesquiquadrate. Spiritual matters influenced her life and goals. The latter planets are in a T-square with those across the horizon which may suggest that the home and relationships undergo upheaval and change, as indeed they did. Annie built a new home in India, a spiritual home which was integral to the Theosophical Society.

Mars is tied to the Moon and Jupiter by sextile, indicating a driving force towards an ideal within the community. With Mars in Taurus and retrograde, a potent struggle ensues with the physical and material world.[4] This is a personal challenge because Mars rules the Aries Ascendant. Organisation, control over disparate forces, co-operation with the divine plan, the will to be and do, and fight, expands an ever growing consciousness.

Example Splay Shape: Hedy Lamarr, Film Star and Inventor

Synopsis

Hedy Lamar, Hollywood star of the 40s and 50s, had both beauty and brains. American audiences apparently gasped the first time she appeared on screen. European audiences also gasped when they saw her running naked through the woods in an earlier Czechoslovakian film called *Ecstasy*.

What is less well known is that Hedy may well be one of the most important inventors of all time. Forgotten for decades, her star shone again in 2014 when she and pianist George Antheil were inducted into the Inventor's Hall of Fame. Together they invented an anti-jamming device for torpedoes, often called frequency hopping but officially known as Spread Spectrum Technology.

The invention is the forerunner of Wifi (wireless local area networking) and GPS (space-based radio navigation system). Most military communications are based on her invention.

In 1997 Lamar and Antheil were honoured with the Electronic Frontier Foundation (EFF) Pioneer Award, and that same year Lamar became the first woman to receive the Bulbie Gnass Spirit of Achievement Award, considered 'The Oscars' of inventing.

Biography

Hedy was born Hedwig Eva Kiesler in Austria of German Jewish parentage. Her film career began in Europe, but upon her marriage to a rich arms dealer, Fritz Mandl, her film career was brought to a halt. Although of Jewish descent, Mandl had connections with the fascist governments of Italy and Germany. Hedy attended many soirees with her husband where the talk was of radio technology and science and particularly armaments and weapons systems. Nobody realised that she was highly intelligent and understood what they were talking about.

Virtually a prisoner in her own home, Hedy escaped amid a time of escalating violence against Jews in Europe. She travelled to the United States where her dark exotic looks found success in films such as *Algiers* and *Samson and Delilah*. Actual movie-making was not enough to stimulate her brain cells, so after a hard day on the film set she would come home and play inventor. She had a dedicated room for science.

Hedy had learned that Allied radio-controlled torpedoes in WW2 could easily be jammed and subsequently fail to hit their target. Hedy became a pioneer in the field of wireless communications, then she and George Antheil received a patent for a radio signalling device. This was a means of manipulating radio frequencies at irregular intervals between transmission and reception to keep enemies from decoding messages. The device used a piano roll to unexpectedly change the frequency.

Originally designed to defeat the German Nazis, the system became an important step in the development of technology to maintain the security of both military communications and cellular phones. Unfortunately Hedy was not instantly recognized for her invention since its wide influence was not understood until decades later.

Hedy was married six times and had three children. She grew rich from film-making but she also spent lavishly, and fell on hard times. She was charged with shop-lifting articles of little value from a drug store on 21 January 1966.

Astrology

Triplicities
Fire: Moon, Venus, Neptune
Air: Jupiter, Uranus
Earth: None
Water: Mercury, Sun, Mars, Saturn, Pluto

Quadruplicities
Cardinal: Saturn, Pluto
Fixed: Moon, Mercury, Sun, Mars, Jupiter, Uranus, Neptune
Mutable: Venus

Houses
Angular: None
Succedent: Moon, Mercury, Sun, Mars, Jupiter, Uranus, Neptune
Cadent: Venus, Saturn, Pluto

Boundary Planets: Jupiter/Saturn, Moon/Mercury, Venus/Uranus

Midpoints to Boundary Planets: Moon/Mercury-Uranus

Mutual Reception: None

Singleton: Venus/Mutable

Hedy's chart has four separate planetary groupings fulfilling a Splay shape and indicating her staunch individuality and non-conformity to what was expected of a movie star: she preferred intellectual conversations to drinking and carousing into the night.

Independence of thought is integral to the Splay shape as is the meaning of the core opposition chart: Moon/Uranus. It is further

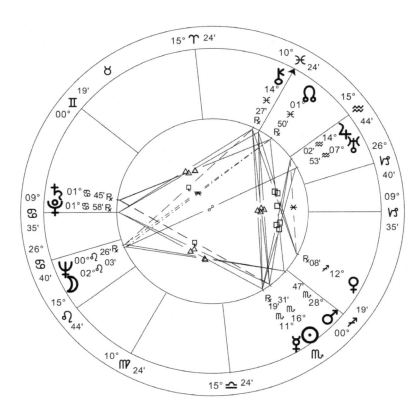

Hedy Lamarr: 9 November 1914, 19:30 CET -1:00
Vienna, Austria 48°N13' 016°E20'

suggesting originality and rebelliousness. The Moon, important because it is the High Focus Planet, rules the Cancer Ascendant which might suggest a strong reliance on self. That Hedy might do so with confidence and self-determination is probably down to the Moon's placement in Leo. The Moon's midpoints are heavy ones however: Saturn/Node, Pluto/Node, Mars/Saturn[5] which shows the depth of the lady under the glamorous image.

The Moon has close links to a further outer planet, Neptune by conjunction. This lifts the individual on to a higher level of consciousness.[6] Jupiter opposite Moon gives farsightedness and a shot of luck by completing the four pronged opposition. All in Leo/Aquarius, signs linked to performance, leadership and science and humanitarianism.

Poured into the 2nd/8th house axis these oppositions suggest financial gains and losses, underpinning the lesson of values. On a higher level it suggests inner illumination, and understanding.

Therefore the central oppositions have power and influence in two distinct areas: film and science. It could also be said that film, though linked with performance, also fell into the field of new technology in early 20th century. Since Neptune co-rules the Midheaven, it links the persona with the career. Jupiter also rules the Midheaven and promises success by its sextile to Venus which itself squares the Midheaven and is indicative of Hedy's beauty, which drove her career.

Venus being a singleton in a mutable sign highlights the Sagittarian drive for freedom to pursue wide-ranging interests. The idealism inherent in this placement, in the 6th house, may be translated into practical hard work, and a need to serve. The square to Chiron in the 10th indicates the exposure of wounds to the world; her reputation was important. Although Hedy bemoaned Hollywood's emphasis on physical appearance, she underwent a great deal of plastic surgery to keep her looks.

On a higher level, Chiron in Pisces and its connection with the symbol of the World Saviour[7] empathises with collective pain. Hedy was able, through musical notation supplied by her colleague George Antheil, to invent a device which saved lives. Emphasis is put on Chiron since it is a singleton in angular houses. Indeed no planets are angular or in Earth signs, which perhaps suggests that much occurred on the mental place and could not find expression or acceptance on the physical plane.

Perseverance was not lacking however, since there is a strong emphasis on fixed signs and succedent houses. Hedy and George produced something so remarkable that its significance was not recognised in 1942. Frequency hopping was a great idea but its time hadn't come. Many inventors on similar lines have since credited the earlier invention by these two extraordinary people.

Chiron connects to Mercury by trine in Scorpio revealing depth of thought, which is amplified by its retrograde motion. Its Grand Trine with the Ascendant and Midheaven is suggestive of her mental gifts and talent for mathematics.[8] Mercury receiving a square aspect from Jupiter supports that talent. Scorpio is further emphasised by the Sun and Mars, also in 5th house. This of course is the house of creativity and performance, the area of life which was the most outwardly prominent. The Scorpio influence can create great highs and great lows which in this case could affect her love affairs and children – which it did.

Mars in domicile is powerful and square the nodes; a planetary contact to the nodes usually paints the individual's life with strong colours. Mars, the god of war, describes Hedy's connection to machines and military; her father's instruction to the young Hedy about the working of machines, and her arms-dealing first husband where she learnt about technology leading to her amazing military invention. Mars trines the all-important Moon, ruler of Hedy's Ascendant, spearheading a drive towards success.

The Sun, associated with the Splay chart, endeavours to draw the disparate areas of the personality into a cohesive whole. In Scorpio, it is done through tests and trials which involve money, sex and power, suggesting such areas were rather challenging throughout Hedy's life and relationships. The Sun is sesquiquadrate both Saturn and Pluto in the isolating 12th house, Saturn rules 7th house, Pluto rules the intercepted Scorpio in 5th house. Her six marriages and several love affairs were indeed challenging, and she spent the greater part of her life alone.

Her birthday on 9th November is celebrated as Inventor's Day in her native Austria.

The Splay Shape: Tripod Variation

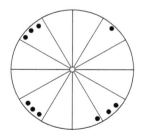

Description

This is a variation of the Splay shape (though Jansky does not make the distinction and also calls the Splay a Tripod). The physical Tripod has three legs and a neck which supports some kind of instrument on top. Astrologically, the Tripod shape has three clusters of planets – not necessarily in conjunction in each group – with a further planet standing alone. The latter becomes the leading or High Focus Planet.

There should be at least 60°⁹ between each cluster of planets though that is the minimum and the ideal is 90° arc of separation. These clusters of planets tend to create either a Grand Trine or a Grand Cross, or both. A Grand Cross brings more challenges into the life, but often gives strength to overcome them. A Grand Trine helps to ease challenges without much effort. A chart becomes extra-dynamic if it has both patterns.

The planet standing alone is considered to be the place to begin analysis. This is then the High Focus Planet, or sometimes called the 'reins' planet – leading the others.[10]

Positive Traits

This shape promises tremendous ability, and perhaps even genius.[11] There could be three distinct areas of interest in life with a certain amount of changeability, but these areas may be linked in some way too. If not then possibly three separate groups of friendships exist, with no obvious connection.

The planet standing alone may well be the foundation of the chart, through which other areas of the chart are channelled. This could show talent in some direction. Certainly there may be something unique or original about the individual. There is usually stability and inner assuredness. The individual works best when feeling grounded; they may even have an interest in real estate or are always seeking ways to anchor their ideas.

Challenging Traits

There could be something secretive about the individual, which might not be deliberate. They may just hold things in different compartments of the mind, and not see any reason for interaction.

Going their own way as they often do, they could also be seen as rather eccentric; they have their own truth. Indeed they do seem to think differently, which can make them out of step with friends, or even society.

They can at times be a little narrow-minded, or fixated upon something which narrows their vision, though this can also suggest tremendous focus.

Example Chart: Franklin Delano Roosevelt, 32nd President of the United States

Synopsis

Franklin Delano Roosevelt – referred to as FDR – was the 32nd President of the United States. A Democrat, he served from 1933 until his death in 1945 – a very difficult time in American history. There was a decline in world economy, though it originated in the United States with the stock market crash, and unemployment rose to unprecedented levels.

In 1939 war began in Europe, which America was loath to enter, until the Japanese strike on a U.S. naval base in Pearl Harbour, Hawaii in 1941. The US had no option but to take up arms in what would become the worst war in history – WW2.

Biography

FDR was born in New York to a wealthy family which included Theodore Roosevelt, 26th President of the United States. FDR studied and practised law, and entered politics in 1910, serving as Assistant Secretary of the Navy under President Woodrow Wilson during WW1.

During a family holiday in 1921 FDR contracted a condition that led to the paralysis of his lower limbs. It may have been poliomyelitis, a viral disease, but more recently it is thought that he may have suffered Guillain-Barre syndrome (GBS) which is a rapid-onset muscle weakness caused by the immune system damaging the peripheral nervous system; sometimes developing weakness of the respiration muscles. Certainly FDR had trouble breathing.

When FDR realised that he would never walk again he gave up politics. He returned to the law and various other hobbies. He was eventually coaxed back to politics in 1928 and was elected Governor of New York.

In 1933 he was elected president and went on to serve an unprecedented four terms, dying in office in 1945. In the early thirties America was in the throes of the Great Depression, where a quarter of the workforce was unemployed and two million people were homeless. Roosevelt blamed the economic crisis on bankers and financiers, the quest for profit, and the self-interest basis of capitalism.

During his presidency the public were not aware that he was unable to walk unaided, as it wasn't reported by the Press. Although his marriage to Eleanor had suffered due to his relationship with another woman, she helped him enormously during his term of office. She often went in his stead and delivered speeches, as if on his behalf.

After the New Deal, the economy began to improve and he was re-elected in 1936. Repealing Prohibition helped, since it brought more jobs in the liquor industry. The economy relapsed again in 1937-39, but was slowly revived again just before the world war.

FDR was noted for his 'fireside chats' a term referring to radio conversations given by him between 1933 and 1944 where he was able to keep the population aware of what was happening economically, and to give them assurance.

Astrology

Triplicities
Fire: None
Air: Mercury, Venus, Mars, Sun
Earth: Jupiter, Saturn, Uranus, Neptune
Water: Moon

Quadruplicities
Cardinal: Moon
Fixed: Venus, Sun, Jupiter, Saturn, Neptune, Pluto
Mutable: Mars, Uranus

Houses
Angular: Moon, Mars
Succedent: Venus, Sun, Jupiter, Saturn, Neptune
Cadent: Mercury, Uranus, Pluto

Reception: Moon/Jupiter, Mercury/Uranus, Venus/Saturn,

Singleton: Moon (Water)

Handle: Uranus/Virgo/12th house

FDR's Tripod-shaped chart has the standard three planetary groupings, and one lone planet – Uranus – in the Eastern hemisphere. This becomes the High Focus Planet giving a flair for innovation.[12] It also refers to

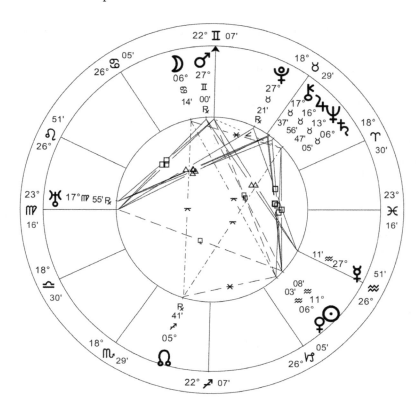

Franklin D Roosevelt: 30 January 1882, 20:45 LMT +4:55:44
Hyde Park, New York 41°N47'05" 073°W56'01"

inter-relatedness and the urge to better environmental conditions as
well as a desire to change the old order.[13] This is what FDR did by
instigating the New Deal in economics.

Whilst seeming gregarious he kept many of his thoughts to himself.
This could be due to the tendency of the Tripod individual to focus his
attention in several different spheres, as well as the 12th house tenancy
of the High Focus Planet. This house linked with Pisces refers to the
World Saviour[14] hinting at the possibility of affecting society on a large
scale – which is how he must have been viewed during the Depression
and WW2 since he was elected to office four times instead of the usual
two terms

The limitation of the 12th house with Uranus retrograde conjunct
the Ascendant also illustrates FDR's loss of mobility. Placed in Virgo,
Uranus and the Ascendant refer to service and indeed one of the first

things FDR did as President was to introduce a series of programs to combat the terrible poverty and unemployment which had devastated the nation. Virgo on the Ascendant can refer to both health issues as well as service of course.

Uranus co-rules the 6th house and is in mutual reception with Mercury in Aquarius in the 6th house, which stresses the importance of humanitarian service. Modern astrological thinking sees Mercury in its exaltation in Aquarius,[15] possibly because Uranus – associated with Aquarius – is seen as the high octave of Mercury. This puts the emphasis on the nervous system, creating a super-charged mentality but also irritation of the nerves and muscles. This could have been linked to Roosevelt's lack of mobility. Mercury's trine to Mars in the 10th house and square to Pluto in the 9th house shows the world a fighting spirit through government and law.

Referring back to the High Focus Uranus, we can see that its trine to Jupiter allowed FDR's luck and unbounded optimism to surface when in office; he urged the American people to view the future with confidence. Jupiter also rules the 4th and 7th houses, describing fortune in family inheritance and partnership.

A trine from Uranus to Chiron and Neptune in the 8th house indicates finances slipping through the fingers. The bulk of his father's estate went to FDR's mother making him dependent upon her financially. Neptune works for the greater good however, and it was repealing the laws on alcohol that helped unemployment.

Completing the planets in Taurus in the 8th house, we see that Saturn threatens to bring tests and trials connected with shared/other people's resources. Indeed, FDR came to the presidency aiming to right the economy. That Saturn is square the Sun is indicative of the heavy burden he carried, as well as the struggles he endured with the Sun's sesquiquadrate Mars. The fact that he was guiding the USA through the dark days of the war is the proof of his great struggle, on a personal and global level.

When the Sun is linked to Mars and Saturn by aspect, or by any other configuration such as reception for instance, a deepening of consciousness often ensues. Since Saturn rules the 6th house, and is involved in a midpoint with the Sun and Neptune, this augured badly for FDR's health.[16] The Sun in Aquarius in its detriment puts the spotlight on others, highlighting group consciousness.

Also in Aquarius in the 5th house resides Venus, strong in its Joy seeking alliances to unite with others for the good of the group. Venus is given a hard time however, by its square and reception with Saturn bestowing discipline through hardship. But blessings come from the sextile both Venus and Sun make to the North Node in Sagittarius in the 3rd house. The node on the fortunate Mars/Jupiter midpoint is an aid to oratory.

Venus and the North Node make a Finger of God connection with the Moon in Cancer in the 10th house. This creates a link with the public. FDR managed to blend the group consciousness of Sun in Aquarius and the symbol of family through the singleton Moon's position in Cancer to reach the people. No doubt the Moon's reception with Jupiter (by exaltation) was an advantage. The 'fire-side' chats on the radio, whilst reaching out to thousands, gave an impression of intimacy.

References

1.   *The Guide to Horoscope Interpretation*, p.104.
2.   *Planetary Patterns*, p.68.
3.   *The Combination of Stellar Influences*, pp 87, 101.
4.   Oken, Alan. *Soul-Centred Astrology*, Bantam Books, 1990, p.292.
5.   *The Combination of Stellar Influences*, pp. 157, 191, 215.
6.   *Soul-Centred Astrology*, p.319.
7.   ibid p.247.
8.   *Christian Astrology*, Regulus, p.78.
9.   *Planetary Patterns*, p.67.
10.   ibid p.68.
11.   ibid p.67.
12.   *Astrology the Sacred Science*, pp.192,139.
13.   *Esoteric Astrology*, p.224.
14.   ibid, p.204.
15.   *Transpersonal Astrology*, p.187.
16.   *The Combination of Stellar Influences*, p.187.

8

The Wedge Shape and its Variation

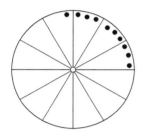

Description

Also referred to as a Bundle shape, the planets are gathered between 90° to 120° of arc.[1] Visually the planets are contained within one third of the chart, leaving two thirds empty. In theory the tighter the planetary group, the greater force, power and magnetism, but this has to be supported by other factors in the chart, such as strength of the planets.

The Wedge starting point differs from other shapes in that the activating point of interpretation is usually a confining square, or maybe even a confining trine between the boundary planets.[2] If an aspect exists between the two boundary planets, be it square or a trine, it is thought to give a more self-contained energy to the shape. A square would naturally be more dynamic, though with greater challenges.

The houses occupied by the boundary planets, their signs and aspects are of importance.

The midpoint and its house position between the two boundary planets is a contributory driving force of the Wedge chart. This includes the house opposite, and any planet falling on the midpoint.

This chart shape is purported to be that of a young soul[3] possibly because there is still so much ground to cover, that is, experiences yet to encounter – note the large 'empty space'. This concept is something that may be borne in mind but with reservation.

Positive characteristics

The Wedge shape seems to crop up infrequently[4] which in itself may suggest a rare type of person, maybe someone who stands apart from the crowd for good or ill. With only a few houses tenanted, the individual tends to work within very specific parameters, giving powerful focus.

Somewhat intense, this person will be a leader rather than a follower, indeed, could be a trailblazer, with certain magnetism. Self-reliant and self-directed, and once interest is established in any pursuit they follow a trajectory that never wavers, with great thoroughness. They are able to build large oaks from little acorns, and tend not to scatter energies. They don't need to rely on others' approval or encouragement, and rely on themselves for decision-making. In fact, they have a way of drawing others into their perspective on life.

They are independent, and deal with life on their own terms, quick to see advantages and able to seize upon anything which may help towards their goals. Goals are usually obsessively pursued, with specialisation in some field since the energy is channelled in one direction.

Challenging Characteristics

Planets within a confining square or trine may indicate a driven individual that remains blind to other people's needs. Self-seeking, they tend to exclude those who aren't essential to their goals.

There may be some discord in co-operating with others, perhaps because of the inability to understand differences, represented by the large space in the chart. Therefore, they may not be interested in what happens outside of their immediate circle. There is usually little ability for small talk.

Since there is often an unwillingness to compromise principles, they are not always understood, perhaps resulting in rejection on either part. Lack of understanding may inhibit empathy. Aloofness may be a trait but possibly through a sense of vulnerability or shyness. Sometimes behaviour can be tantamount to inertia until something catches their interest, then they are galvanised into action.

The empty space of the chart can be experienced through another person if their planets should occupy the relevant houses.

This may not be the easiest of shapes since the individual needs to find something specific on which to focus, otherwise they may feel like an outsider. Withdrawal from life could result, though positively this could be time spent on some area of creativity.

Associated Planet: Saturn seems fitting since it works within narrow parameters, creating limitation, but also discipline, stability and focus, steadily and towards a specific goal.

Example Wedge Chart: Harrison Ford, Actor

Synopsis

Harrison Ford has been a very big box office draw in film, and though quiet and unassuming in real life, he is dynamic on the big screen.

Although he became interested in acting at an early age, he didn't create a stir in the film world until he was in his mid-thirties. In between small film roles he worked successfully as a carpenter to the stars.

After his part as Hans Solo in *Star Wars*, he hardly looked back, appearing in the Indiana Jones series and as agent Jack Ryan in several thrillers.

Biography

Much of his childhood was difficult in the sense that he felt like a loner and somewhat distanced from his young peers. His mother was Jewish and his father Catholic, which gave him the opportunity to experience different religious denominations. This taught him to question the world about him. Inner self-esteem and a sense of self was the result, although he felt like an outsider until he discovered drama, and subsequently film.

Once he decided on his career he displayed great tenacity in pursuing his dream, despite setbacks. It was a long time coming though, and he filled the time by studying carpentry.

Although he was in various films throughout his twenties, he was 35 years of age before he became a big star. He was always himself in real life and never tried to ingratiate himself, which did not always go down well in interviews. Much of this was due to his need to be true to what he felt inside. This gained him a reputation for truculence, and being difficult to work with, but he always wanted to play fair by his conscience and wouldn't take a film role, generally, if the part did not agree with him.

He loves acting in film, but reached the pinnacle of his profession on his own terms; neither does he really fit into the Hollywood mould. He did not fall in line with other people's expectations, or bow to other people's wishes, and remained independent and always himself.

Many of his films are adventure stories like the Indiana Jones series, where he did most of his own stunts. Since they are based on action he felt he wouldn't have much to do if he let a stuntman do his work. Among some of his best known films are *Witness, Blade Runner, The Fugitive, The Mosquito Coast* and *Frantic*.

His ranch in Jackson, Wyoming is 800 acres, half of which has been donated as a nature reserve. In 1998, he was chosen as *People* magazine's Sexiest Man Alive. He was listed in the 2001 Guinness Book of Records as the richest male actor. He is a very private man and rarely gives interviews. A sense of his need for freedom is reflected in his love of flying.

Harrison has been married three times, the first to Mary Marquardt, whom he met at college, then Melissa Mathison, who wrote the script for the block buster film, *E. T. The Extra-Terrestrial*. He is now married to Calista Flockhart who starred in the legal drama *Ally McBeal*. He is both a father and grandfather.

Astrology

Triplicities
Fire: Mars, Pluto
Air: Venus, Saturn, Uranus
Earth: Neptune
Water: Moon, Mercury, Sun, Jupiter

Quadruplicities
Cardinal: Moon, Mercury, Sun, Jupiter
Fixed: Mars, Pluto
Mutable: Venus, Saturn, Uranus, Neptune

Houses
Angular: Moon, Sun, Jupiter
Succedent: Mars
Cadent: Mercury, Venus, Saturn, Uranus, Neptune

Singleton: Mars/Succedent

Boundary planets: Uranus and Neptune

Uranus/Neptune midpoint: 0.19 Leo, 10th house

The tenanted four houses at the top of the chart make a typical Wedge shape, bounded by a Uranus and Neptune trine. With such

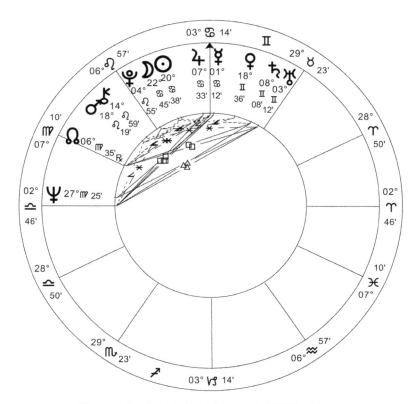

Harrison Ford: 13 July 1942, 11:41 CWT +5:00
Chicago, Illinois 41°N51' 087°W39'

an empty expanse of chart there may be a feeling of uncertainty when functioning in an unfamiliar terrain. At school Harrison felt something of an outcast, and suffered bullying. Nevertheless, with the emphasis on cardinal and angular planets, there is purposeful direction in the chosen career – in his case it was acting.

Uranus and Neptune often show up as boundary planets in the charts of scientists, psychics or those who make some kind of global impact. The film which brought Harrison to the public eye was also based on science of the fictional variety – *Star Wars*. In real life, Harrison is vice-chair of Conservative International, an American non-profit organisation which endeavours to combine the services and benefits of science to find global solutions to global problems regarding water, food and air.

Judgement can begin with the faster moving boundary planet, Uranus, suggesting mental acuity in Gemini with a philosophical turn of mind in the 9th house. Ford studied philosophy at university. A conjunction to Saturn associated with the Wedge chart shows a certain amount of struggle in life, and questioning of established rules and beliefs. Saturn ruling the 4th house has connections with the environment. Harrison assists the Archaeological Institute of America by increasing public awareness of archaeology and preventing looting and the illegal antiquities trade. It was his films based on archaeologist Indiana Jones that sparked his real life interest in archaeology.

Incidentally carpentry – his stop-gap job – is ruled by Saturn.[5]

Saturn and Uranus are semi-square the Sun and Moon in Cancer. Whilst Cancer, like the Wedge shape, prefers a familiar terrain, the connection with the former planets indicates that established ideas will be questioned. With Sun/Moon in Cancer in the 10th the ability to tune into mass-consciousness contributes to success in the career. Particularly pertinent since the strong Moon in domicile rules the Midheaven.

A great sign of success is given by the exalted Jupiter in the vicinity of the Midheaven. Mercury on the other side creates a midpoint of intellect and achievement. Mars joins in with a semi-square indicating a forceful speaker and a man of action, emphasised by its singleton status.

Neptune, at the other end of the Wedge boundary, in Virgo, gains strength by its position on the Ascendant. Compassion together with the fantasy world of film is the result. In detriment, this may have caused some earlier conflict. He was very shy in school, and often felt like a fish out of water, to coin a phrase!

The midpoint Uranus/Neptune 0.19 Leo/10th house, is semi-square Venus, albeit widely, indicating acute sensitivity. Venus in Gemini, the ruler of the Libra Ascendant, makes the issues of the 9th house of even greater importance; such as the search for truth, and understanding of the laws of nature. Yet there is fun associated with Venus too, and in interviews, Harrison laughs readily and is talkative on issues he knows about.

Libra, which describes deliberate thought before action, endeavours to give balanced judgement, and impartiality. Harrison always chose his parts carefully; there were no quick decisions for the sake of being in work.

Venus semi-square Pluto gives him magnetism and perhaps that rather mesmerising voice. Venus sextile Mars suggests easy contact with others. Since both planets rule 1st/7th, and 2nd/8th houses, marriage and money should flow easily. Mars in Leo is competitive and courageous and its semi-square to both the Ascendant and Midheaven shows that action can burst forth through the rather relaxed exterior.

The Wedge Chart: Fanhandle Variation

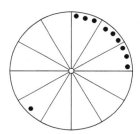

Description

This is a variation of a Wedge chart. Nine planets are positioned within circa 90° of arc. The tenth planet is usually placed almost opposite the main group, though a chart can still qualify as a Fanhandle if it appears visually to stand apart from the other planets. This is the High Focus Planet which channels the energy of the planets in the main group. As usual it should be examined in relation to its strength, sign, house position and aspects, as well as midpoints.

A two handle variation can also occur. This should only be considered if the main group of planets are within tight parameters.

The midpoints linked to the boundary planets are also important. The house axis of the midpoint will be emphasised, and particularly so if there is a planet that falls on that midpoint, irrespective of whether the planet is the Handle (High Focus Planet) or not.

Positive Traits

The Fanhandle follows a trajectory that doesn't waver; it stays focused, with great intensity. Self-reliant and focused goals appear more easily accessible than the typical Wedge, usually through the Handle. This person tends to associate with like-minded people, and, if aiming for the same goals, a gathering of powerful energies could occur. There is an ability to fire others with enthusiasm, since there is often much self belief. This individual prefers to deal with life on their own terms.

Like the typical Wedge this shape augers a specialist in some field, which could be revealed by the signs/houses involved. It seems to contain something within to offer the world outside.[6]

Challenging Traits

Great belief in their own ideas can alienate others because this person does not try to win people over with charm. Friendships may be few, but often firm and loyal. More likely, they are able to steer their own course in life through self-motivation without relying on others.

Not one to waste time they don't consider small talk an asset, and this does not always make for great popularity. Nevertheless, they are usually quick to see advantages and to seize upon anything which may further their goals.

The energy poured into their chosen subject is awesome and may be obsessively pursued, as these people usually have all the information they need to hand.

Example Fanhandle Chart: Sir Hugh Dowding, Air Chief Marshall

Synopsis

The Battle of Britain in WW2 was led by R.A.F Fighter Command and masterminded by Air Chief Marshall Sir Hugh Dowding. The Battle of Britain lasted from 10 July to 31 October 1940. It is chiefly due to the Air Chief Marshall's vision and judgement that invasion was stemmed at the tide.

Dowding learned to fly in 1914, and easily grasped scientific and technical principles. He felt the loss of his pilots keenly and whilst others might have referred to having 'lost four planes', he always said he had 'lost four sons'.

Resistance to conventional thought was at the back of his many disputes with authority. He liked to think and prove things for himself, and questioned orders. He was straightforward, practical, frugal and abstemious. Serious at work, he was more jovial socially.

Biography

In 1937, convinced that war with Nazi Germany was inevitable, Dowding pushed for the development of the Royal Air Force, as well as radar. He organised fighter cover in May 1940 with Vice Marshall Keith Park for the British Expeditionary Force at Dunkirk.

RAF Fighter Command was in deepest France trying to stop the Germans overrunning the country. France was desperate for reinforcement in its own fight against the Luftwaffe and Churchill was about to give in to French demand when Dowding persuaded him that the loss of resources in their own battle would most probably lead to the defeat of Britain.

The surprising side to this rather dour man was his interest in spiritualism and reincarnation. He wrote several books on spiritual subjects. He also wrote of meeting dead 'RAF boys' in his sleep – spirits who flew fighters from mountain-top runways made of light. It is thought that his interest in spiritualism forced him out of his position as head of fighter command, and that is why he received less recognition than he deserved.

Dowding sent a letter of condolence to all those who wrote to him. One of the widows was Muriel Whiting whose husband, Max, had died during a bombing mission over Eastern Europe. She was hoping to enlist Dowding's help to find out from the Air Ministry the actual circumstances of her husband's death. When Dowding received her letter, he happened to see a medium around the same time. Muriel Whiting's dead husband Max came through and suggested he meet Mrs Whiting.

They met and fell in love and married and she proved to be a great influence on his life, persuading him to give up game shooting and become a vegetarian. They were both members of the Theosophical Society.

Astrology

Triplicities
Fire: Mercury
Air: Jupiter
Earth: Venus, Sun, Saturn, Uranus, Neptune, Pluto
Water: Moon, Mars

Quadruplicities
Cardinal: Moon, Mercury, Mars
Fixed: Venus, Sun, Saturn, Neptune, Pluto
Mutable: Jupiter, Uranus

Houses
Angular: Venus, Jupiter, Saturn, Neptune, Pluto
Succedent: Mars, Uranus
Cadent: Moon, Mercury, Sun

Reception: None

Handle: Uranus/Virgo/2nd

Boundary Planets: Mercury (leading), Moon (Trailing)

Mercury/Moon midpoint: 10:34 Gemini

Singletons: Mercury (Fire), Jupiter (Air)

The chart may be classed as a Fanhandle since the main group of planets are within 90° of arc. Uranus, which represents the handle, only touches 50° separation, nevertheless, it stands out visually and this is may well be considered a Fanhandle shape.

The Fanhandle spirit of certainty, slight aloofness and dedication to a goal describes Dowding very well. Despite opposition, he was confident in his judgement. He dealt with life on his own terms as indeed the Fanhandle type is wont to do. It certainly took guts to stand up to Churchill, and point out a better way of doing things.

Uranus, the sky god, ruled over the terrain that Dowding also commanded. Uranus is linked with science and technical matters too, as well as a new way of doing things.[7] The Air Chief Marshall was quick to grasp technical details.

In Virgo, Uranus engineers practical service as well as streamlines, organizes and economises.[8] Certainly Dowding was very down to earth. In the 2nd house, Uranus indicates that his values were different from those around him, especially since the planet is retrograde. This makes him think things through more deeply.

Uranus trine Saturn and Neptune bestows both practicality and vision (and being open to the spirit realm), and the trine to Venus in Taurus gives excellent valuation and judgement, and luck of course.

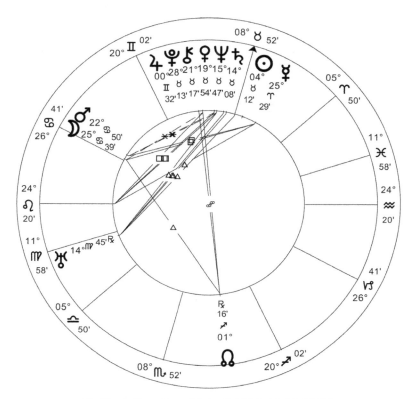

Sir Hugh Dowding: 24 April 1882, 12:30 GMT
Moffat, Scotland 55°N20' 003°W27'

The strong Venus in its own sign rules the 10th house of career. It becomes militarised by its separating conjunction with Saturn and applying sextile to Mars, bringing two malefics together. It was through struggle and war that Dowding came to prominence.

The midpoints involving Uranus are the Sun with Mercury and the Moon; the latter two planets are important since they are the boundary planets. This describes independent, advanced thinking, far-reaching plans and good oration.[9] Uranus is also on the Midheaven/Mars midpoint indicating independent action.[10]

Saturn conjunct the Midheaven moderates the wilful behaviour of Uranus. Dowding ruled with an earnestness and solemnity that did not always endear him to others – although he was popular with his pilots. He was his own man and did not try to please anyone. He did not play politics, he was very straight. Saturn in the 10th traditionally heralds a fall from grace[11] and of course this occurred despite having kept the Huns at bay. Dowding was removed from office soon after the Battle of Britain. The official reason, and indeed it may have been quite accurate, was that his expertise on air technology was needed elsewhere. (Nothing to do with his spiritual views then!)

The full 10th house is indicative of someone who has the opportunity to take responsibility, and Dowding certainly did that. Chiron is there too which may indicate a wound to his reputation (due to his removal after masterminding the Battle of Britain perhaps?)

Also in practical and steadfast Taurus, and the other side of the Midheaven, stands the Sun in its Joy in the 9th house. This gives strong principles and an understanding of higher truths. The Sun only has a conjunction with Mercury suggesting standing alone. In a sense this is where Dowding's destiny was firmly linked with Britain's, since in the summer of 1940, Britain stood alone against the enemy (other countries having been defeated). The Sun rules the Leo Ascendant which tests the individual to stand on their own two feet and take command, which is of course what Dowding did to a superlative degree.

The Ascendant degree links into a T-square with the nodes, Venus, Jupiter and Pluto which shows great undertakings. That Dowding had a huge effect upon world fate is certainly true. The nodes indicate fate, fortune and the public. The North Node also stands apart from all the planets, including the handle planet, and this has to be considered more fully. In Sagittarius, this shows the far-reaching effect that is possible in the sphere of travel, and in the 4th house, the guarding of home and country. Jupiter opposes the North Node as well as it conjuncts the South Node, which in a sense creates faith in abilities.

Jupiter in Gemini, its detriment, now strives to understand the true nature of man's duality,[12] hence Dowding's interest in the physical and spiritual sides of life. Jupiter's singleton status in Air emphasises this idea. Both Jupiter and Pluto are linked to the Moon and Mars in Cancer. The Moon separates from the conjunction of Mars and applies by sextile to Jupiter and Pluto. These planets might suggest the 'great or divine mother' on a wide ranging scale described by the 11th and 12th houses. Dowding was indeed like the veritable mother hen since his flyers were called 'Dowding's chicks'.

References

1. *Planetary Patterns*, p.5.
2. ibid p.51.
3. ibid, p.53.
4. ibid p.49.
5. Ramesey, W. 1653 *Astrologia Restaurata*, or *Astrology Restored,* printed for Robert White: London pp. 050, 054. (Also Lilly, W. 1647, *Christian Astrology* in 1985 by Regulus, London p.94.)
6. *The Guide to Horoscope Interpretation*, p.30.
7. *Esoteric Astrology*, p.244.
8. Lake, Gina. *Symbols of the Soul*, Endless Satsang Foundation, p.109.
9. *The Combination of Stellar Influences,* pp.94/95.
10. ibid pp.168/9.
11. *Christian Astrology*, p.55.
12. *Esoteric Astrology, p.365.*

9

Mixed and Irregular Chart Shapes

Some charts do not fit into the seven basic shapes or their variants, or rather not entirely. Indeed, some charts cannot quite make up their minds which shapes they truly are; often they are a mixture of two.

Rather than this being a problem, these wayward charts should be a spur to interpretation. Indeed a planet removed from the ideal shape – whichever is under designation – can show the way into the chart. And naturally this is the aim, rather than making a chart fit into a particular shape. More tools become available for the astrologer to use. Examples will follow to clarify this further.

Such charts claim no superiority over others, nor are they inferior. They just provide a puzzle to unravel. Some detective work is needed; the clues are there.

Firstly decide which shape the chart almost fits, and then examine the planet creating the difference. That planet, falling outside the ideal shape, becomes significant in the interpretation. A significant planet therefore, is one which falls outside the ideal shape but still retains the integrity of the shape.[1] This then, paradoxically, becomes the High-Focus Planet.

In the case of charts seemingly creating two strong contenders for its shape, then a decision has to be made which shape dominates, determined visually or by counting the degrees. Or if it is somehow still impossible to decide, then meld the two together. The following charts, biographies and abbreviated analysis provide a few examples.

Locomotive Further Variation: David Lloyd George
Prime Minister 1916-1922

Brief Biography

The last Liberal Prime Minister of Great Britain, David Lloyd George, was a great reformer, as well as helping to steer the country towards victory in WW1.

Since he came to politics from the working classes Lloyd George was something of an outsider. He was viewed with suspicion by the long established gentry in government. Members of Parliament were not paid until 1911 which precluded those without a private income from becoming involved in politics.

He became Chancellor of the Exchequer under the Herbert Henry Asquith Liberal government, and pushed forward the Old Age Pensions Act of January 1909, providing social insurance that was to be financed by the land and income taxes. In this position he instituted many other reforms that founded the modern welfare state.

Astrology

Triplicities
Fire: Moon, Neptune
Air: Mercury, Venus, Jupiter, Saturn, Uranus
Earth: Sun, Mars, Pluto
Water: None

Quadruplicities
Cardinal: Sun, Jupiter, Saturn, Neptune
Fixed: Mercury, Venus, Mars, Pluto
Mutable: Moon, Uranus

Houses
Angular: Mercury, Venus, Sun
Succedent: Moon, Jupiter, Saturn, Uranus, Neptune
Cadent: Mars, Pluto

Boundary Planets: Jupiter/Uranus (Saturn) 21.49 Leo (7th house)

Midpoints to B.P. : Saturn 5.31 Libra by semi-square

Mutual Reception: Venus/Aquarius – Saturn/Libra

Singleton/s: Saturn outside boundary line Jupiter/Uranus
                Pluto/Cadent

The shape of this chart will explain how a planet falls away from the designated shape – in this case a Locomotive – but it still retains the integrity of a Locomotive.

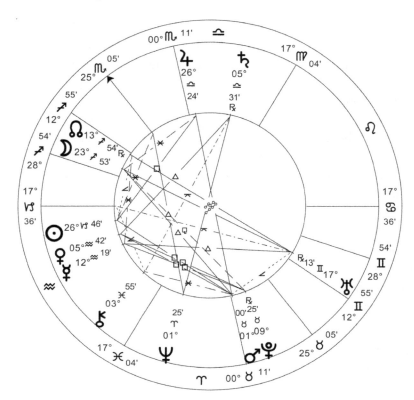

David Lloyd George: 17 January 1863, 07:55 UT
Manchester, England 53°N30' 002°W15'

The two boundary planets – Saturn and Uranus – do not have the customary trine between them since they are 108° apart. There is however a trine between Jupiter and Uranus, albeit wide, which drives Saturn outside the new boundary line. Now standing apart of the main frame, Saturn could become the High Focus Planet[2] since it introduces something new into the picture, and therefore invites interpretation.

Once the astrologer becomes familiar with all the seven shapes, and their variants, it will be easier to spot the planet that stands apart or away from the designated description.

In the chart of Lloyd George, Saturn stands outside the containing trine between Jupiter and Uranus, the first indication of an individual who stood on the edge of society. This description exactly fits Lloyd George, who was an outsider in politics as he came from the poorer classes at a time when Members of Parliament were drawn from the moneyed classes. That Lloyd George was able to fight his corner against prejudice and snobbery is described by Saturn's extraordinary strength in the chart. It is in its exaltation as well as trine and in mutual reception with Venus, a benefic. Saturn in Libra represents justice. In 1883 Lloyd George took up a career in the law.

Venus conjunct Mercury hints at superb oratorical ability. In Aquarius, the two planets instil humanitarian, reformative ideals. Since the chart emphasises the intellectual Air, with Water absent, Lloyd-George's modus operandi was indeed through the power of the mind and word.

Saturn in the 8th house of death, transformation, and shared resources describes the area of life which propelled Lloyd George before the public. He dealt with a case of burial rights and won, which made his name.

Saturn rules the Capricorn Ascendant which can spur the native on to the heights of material ambition or elevate spiritual consciousness.[3] A sense of responsibility and serving others may be qualities marking the individual's higher state of consciousness. Lloyd George never forgot the poverty experienced by the working classes, and fought to get a better welfare state for the ordinary man.

Saturn's prestige does fall however, because the opposition to Neptune elicited a scandal in finance. Across the 2nd/8th houses, it might be called insider-dealing these days. Saturn inconjunct Chiron in Pisces in the 1st house reveals a wound to his personal identity. Indeed, coming from a poor background he was set apart from the rich and titled people he mixed with in Parliament.

Completing the planets in the 1st house is the Sun in Capricorn, indicating that success will come through the force of the personality. There was no doubt that Lloyd-George's personality created the strength that bore him towards great heights in life – helped liberally of course by the aspects to the squares of Mars and Jupiter which would further that ambition.

Mars, the god of War, is associated with the Locomotive chart. Britain became fully mobilized under Lloyd George in WW1, as he took on the role of the Minister of Armaments. Yet Mars in its detriment in Taurus, indicates struggles which fuelled his oratorical battles in the House of Commons. The square to Venus adds charm, and the conjunction to Pluto, a singleton (cadent) reveals the annihilating quality of his speeches.

Jupiter, as leading boundary planet by virtue of his trine to Uranus, is in Libra and the 8th house as is Saturn, the High Focus Planet. Here Jupiter will also stand for justice and transformation and push for fairness in all matters, with the ability to discern the needs of others, making an excellent diplomat.

Whilst Jupiter leads with high ideas, Uranus, the trailing planet, brings reformative tendencies and highlights the spoken word in Gemini, giving an ability to play to an audience in the 5th house. The road would not be easy because Saturn forms a midpoint to Jupiter and Uranus, the boundary planets. Reforms did not often go down well with the government elite – the House of Lords.

Jupiter brings luck to public affairs since it is sextile the Moon in Sagittarius, and envisions the goals ahead with consciousness of purpose. The Moon with the nodes and Uranus, the trailing planet, may well indicate ability for self promotion in an original way, supported by the trine to Mercury, planet of communication.

See-Saw Further Variation: King Ludwig II of Bavaria

Brief Biography

Ludwig II, King of Bavaria, was born at a time when the principalities of Germany had not yet united into an integrated nation state.

Ludwig was a dreamer and idealist rather than a pragmatist, living in his own mythological and musical fantasy world. On becoming king in 1864 he arranged to meet his favourite composer, Richard Wagner, to offer him patronage. Wagner accepted and became a resident of Munich, flourishing as a composer. However, his flamboyant and lavish lifestyle was disliked by the State and he was banished only a year later.

Ludwig had one brother, Otto, who was certified mad, despite having served in the army and reaching quite a high rank. Ludwig too was certified mad just before his death. His lack of interest in affairs of state, eccentric behaviour and bankrupting the exchequer by building castles – in the air, or at least at high altitudes – propelled him down the slippery slope.

The king might have impoverished himself and the State when

he built his fairy-tale castles but nowadays tourists flock to visit them, and have put back the coins in the exchequer - many times over. One of Ludwig's castles, Neuschwanstein above the village of Hohenswchwangau, Southern Bavaria, was the inspiration for Walt Disney's castle in the animated film *The Sleeping Beauty*.

Astrology

Triplicities
Fire: Uranus, Pluto
Air: Moon, Mars, Saturn, Neptune
Earth: Mercury, Venus, Sun, Jupiter
Water: None

Quadruplicities
Cardinal: Uranus, Pluto
Fixed: Mars, Jupiter, Saturn, Neptune
Mutable: Moon, Mercury, Venus, Sun

Houses
Angular: Sun, Neptune
Succedent: Mercury, Venus, Uranus, Pluto
Cadent: Moon, Mars, Jupiter, Saturn

Boundary planets: Moon/Sun, Venus/Saturn

Mutual Reception: None

Singleton: None

This is a See-Saw shape, yet it could also pass for a Splay with three apparent aggregations of planets. Such a combination describes someone who longs to relate, but on his own terms. Indeed, he was an individualist and did not fit into what the State expected of a king. Crowds terrified him and he hated to be stared at. His friends and lovers were fleeting; he did try to marry but preferred a platonic relationship with the sister of his intended. The outer expressions of his inner dream world were music and art.

In both See-Saw and Splay charts it is the core opposition that is the trigger for interpretation. But there isn't one – at least not between two planets. The nearest contender is Neptune on the cusp of the 10th

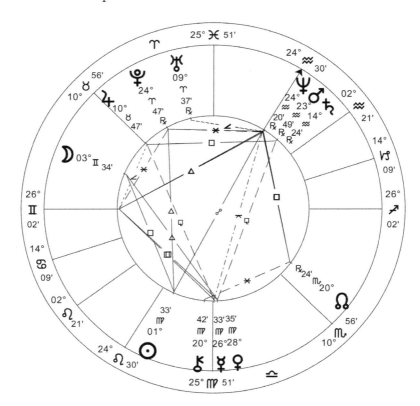

King Ludwig ll: 24 August 1845, 23:35 LMT -00:46:16
Munich, Germany 48°N08' 011°E34'

house, highlighting the MC/IC axis, with Mars tagging along for the ride. This immediately concurs with the king's reputation as a dreamy, visionary individual who found solace in fantasy, as well as isolation. Whilst the Mars/Neptune conjunction can point to an inspirational and idealistic nature, it suggests at the same time a restriction on outer activity. Indeed, the inner life was always most important to Ludwig. With the building of his castles and living the mythology integral to Wagner's music, Ludwig created his own world.

Three planets in Aquarius emphasise objectivity, decentralisation and group awareness and indeed Ludwig found personal contacts difficult and preferred to think on a wider and higher level. Neptune is semi-square Uranus, which again shows a mind transported into soaring realms. The group aspect of Aquarius perhaps comes to the fore through rulership of the 9th and 10th houses, which appoints him king and head of the church. With Saturn in Aquarius, ruling the 6th and 7th houses, he gave much employment to the common people.

The aforesaid planets are in the 9th house of the higher mind, suggesting oppression and instability too. Does this make the king mad? The condition is not easily defined except that we look askance at people who are out of step with others. Indeed Ludwig was very sensitive and found living in the mundane world very difficult.

Neptune and Mars on the MC/IC line influence the parental line, and are also in T-square with the nodes over the 6th/12th houses indicated in health. The Wittelsbach family from which Ludwig descended had a reputation for eccentricity.

The Sun is linked to the MC/IC line since it is in the 4th house and conjunct the IC. In Virgo, on a higher level, inner spiritual reality is sensed[4] which again moves the king to explore his inner life. Perhaps building castles, almost in the air, was like the Egyptians building pyramids to bring themselves closer to the divine.

The Sun square the Moon shows further disquiet between the inner and outer person, and perhaps feeling trapped in the physical world with the Moon in the 12th house. Sensitivity comes with the Moon in Gemini in a hidden house, but also changeability as well as versatility. The power that he had, however, can be seen from the Sun's trine to Pluto, but an outer planet is hardly grounding.

And yet three planets in Virgo do show an ability to put ideas into action, for it is a sign of practical application. That there was great creative flair comes from the conjunction of Mercury and Venus. In Virgo detail would be paramount of course. Since Mercury rules the Ascendant and is in the 5th house with a Venus that is helped a little out from detriment by being in its Joy, it shows where Ludwig's heart really lay. In the theatre – which again has little connection with reality.

Chiron in Virgo conjunct Mercury may indeed show something awry with the mentality, and together with Mercury and Venus they all square the Ascendant affecting the mind and personality.

There is no doubt that Ludwig was highly creative, and perhaps in touch with the divine as many great artists seem to be. Ludwig's life was a mystery, most of all to himself.

Bucket Further Variation: Wernher Von Braun, Physicist

Brief Biography

Wernher von Braun, a German aristocrat who led the way in the field of rocketry, took the United States to the Moon. He was the chief architect of the Saturn V launch vehicle which on 20 July 1969 took the Apollo 11 crew heavenward.

Von Braun became a national figure and gave many lectures to the American public on the advantages of space travel. He wrote several books, among them *Conquest of the Moon* and *Space Travel – A History*. But it all began in Germany, during WW2. It was he who masterminded the V2 long range ballistic missile, a weapon of war. The V2 rocket was sent over London and parts of Belgium in 1944, with devastating effect. Thousands of people died as a result, but even more people died (slave labour) building the rockets. Launched from mobile units in occupied Europe, London was attacked on 8th September 1944. Each rocket was 14 metres (46ft) high, powered by a liquid ethanol fuel, and equipped with an automatic guiding system.

Towards the end of WW2, his team chose to surrender to the Americans rather than Russian forces. The USA overlooked his past connection with the Nazi party since the space race was on – against the Russians. Von Braun and his team began designing US ballistic missiles and settled in Huntsville, Alabama. Some years later Von Braun became the Director of NASA's new Marshall Space Flight Centre.

Nobody before had pushed the boundaries of space so far. His enormous contribution to space exploration buried his involvement with the perpetrators of unequalled horrors.

Astrology

Triplicities
Fire: Mercury, Sun, Jupiter
Air: Mars, Uranus, Pluto
Earth: Moon, Saturn
Water: Venus, Neptune

Quadruplicities
Cardinal: Mercury, Sun, Neptune
Fixed: Moon, Saturn, Uranus
Mutable: Venus, Mars, Jupiter, Pluto

Houses
Angular: Venus, Pluto
Succedent: Mercury, Sun, Neptune,
Cadent: Moon, Mars, Jupiter, Saturn, Uranus

Boundary planets: Uranus/Neptune

Uranus/Neptune Midpoint: 26.48 Aries in the 11th house

Reception: Mercury/Mars

Singleton: None

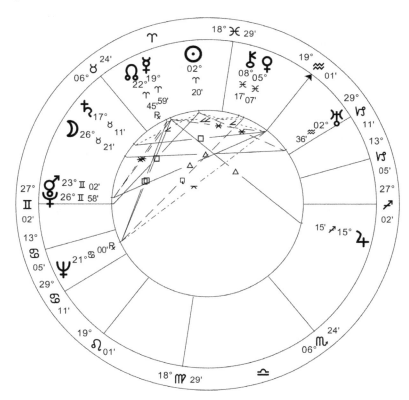

Wernher von Braun: 23 March 1912, 09:15 CET -1:00
Wyrzysk, Poland 53°N10' 017°E15'

The chart is a variation of the Bucket because Jupiter, the handle, is only 45° degrees away from its nearest planetary neighbour Uranus – rather than the usual 60° degrees. Visually of course, Jupiter does stand out.

Jupiter in Sagittarius suggests far reaching aims in the area of travel or religion. Von Braun's long-term vision pushed the boundaries of space travel. The highest quality of Sagittarius is bringing different components of an issue or project towards a common aim.[5]

In the 6th house of work and service, Jupiter describes Von Braun's service to two governments: Germany and America. Jupiter's semi-square to Uranus in Aquarius in the 9th house is indicative of innovations in far distance travel, and originality of mind. With Jupiter's sextile to the Midheaven success is promised. The intellect is sharp with Jupiter trine Mercury and North Node in pioneering Aries.

The Greater Benefic positioned outside the boundary planets Uranus and Neptune, indicates that his urge for travel transcended the bounds of Earth's gravity. Outer planets awaken the human spirit from the darkness and limitation of human thought to the grandeur and freedom of cosmic concepts.

The Uranus/Neptune midpoint at 26.48 Aries falls close to the North Node in Aries indicating a fateful life. Mercury in this sign in the 11th house proposes the ability to cultivate new, original ideas. Mental agility is enhanced by Mercury's sextile to Mars, and mutual reception.

Mercury rules the Ascendant and with the square to Neptune this makes a T-square indicating imagination, compassion and rendering mass service. Neptune in Cancer suggests bringing down spirituality on the material plane.[6] His mind may have been on a higher plane, but it appears he had difficulty in dealing with a simple home drill!

Mars in Gemini brings conflict between opposing ideas. Linked to Pluto on the Ascendant it suggests conviction, power and influence. He also had to wrestle with formidable forces. He was imprisoned by the Gestapo for his reluctance to turn his rocket into a weapon (V2), an act which could have sealed his fate. Both Mars and Pluto rule the 6th house of service and slavery, as well as ill-health. Von Braun developed cancer of the bowel.

That the current life was one of power struggles is further indicated by Pluto's square to the Sun in Aries, which shows the courage to explore new vistas and initiate new enterprises with leadership and inspiration. Sun rules Leo on the 4th house cusp, and in its exalted position describes his aristocratic background.

The Sun in Aries cuts through barriers, and on a higher level paves the way for others. Von Braun had wanted to land on the Moon himself, but he was too old when the time came. That he worked with large groups is shown by the emphasis on the 11th house and the Sun's sextile to Uranus. With his gift of organisation he was able to connect easily with people on a large scale.

Note that the Moon in the chart links to the two boundary planets, albeit widely: a sextile to Neptune and a trine to Uranus. The Moon in Taurus describes von Braun's ability as a builder (of rockets). In the 12th house, drawn to the multitudes and behind the scenes work, and with fixed star *Algol* seems to have described the suffering of thousands in making the V2.

Also in Taurus in the 12th house is Saturn, which indicates that the desire for material satisfaction is transmuted to aspiration to build something of value for the common good. But there still may be constraint by material circumstances where freedom is lacking. Von Braun used the money from the government to build his rockets – initially on the backs of slave labour in the Third Reich.

Saturn is semi-square the Sun which in turn is square Pluto, as well as having a wide square to Mars. Life challenges may be of various kinds but often involve loss, death of a loved one or the seamier side of life, as working for the Nazi party, albeit reluctantly.

Von Braun was very young when responsibility was thrust upon him, and the test and trials not only involved the relentless research into aeronautics, but with life and death situations. He made both the physical journey to the outer reaches of space through his rockets, and the spiritual journey through studying world religions.

Saturn links to Venus by semi-square indicating success in the foregoing matters, especially since Venus is exalted in Pisces, the 10th house bestowing good luck in career.

References
1.   *Planetary Patterns*, p.30.
2.   ibid p.5.
3.   *Esoteric Astrology*, pp.163, 169.
4.   ibid p.271.
5.   ibid pp.178, 258.
6.   ibid p.219.

Appendix

Dignity/Debility

A planet in domicile or exaltation is said to act with strength and follows its usual line of activity. However, when a planet is in detriment or fall, it is said to be weak, at least traditionally speaking. The so-called weakness may be more relevant in horary or decumbiture (medical) charts. In nativities, detriment and fall may not always act adversely, just hinting that a different way of expression is needed.

It is quite possible that a planet in detriment and fall suggests challenging steps towards achieving a deeper consciousness. The planetary debility will encounter more tests since the individual may have to discover a new way or expressing certain energies when first attempts at some kind of activity does not initially yield the best results. Some examples with Mars in Libra, its detriment, will eventually illustrate to the individual that good connections with others needs diplomacy rather than brute force or too much assertion. Or Saturn in Leo, its detriment, has to learn to rise above an adverse environment rather than yield to it. Mercury in Pisces where it is in detriment and fall has to rise above environmental pressures that impinge upon the personality, through which he or she learns compassion, detachment and identifying with something greater.

Planet	Domicile	Exaltation	Detriment	Fall
The Moon	Can	Tau	Cap	Sco
Mercury	Gem & Vir	Vir	Sag & Pis	Pis
The Sun	Leo	Aries	Aq	Lib
Mars	Aries & Sco	Cap	Lib & Tau	Can
Jupiter	Sag & Pis	Can	Gem & Vir	Cap
Saturn	Cap & Aq	Lib	Can & Leo	Aries
Uranus	Aq	Sco	Leo	Tau
Neptune	Pis	Leo	Vir	Aq
Pluto	Sco	Pis	Tau	Vir

Dispositors

The *dispositor* is a planet in whose sign another planet is located in the natal chart and which resident planet gains strength when its dispositor is strong. The final dispositor is a planet that disposits all the other planets because it is placed in the sign that it rules. In charts where there is mutual reception, there is no final dispositor, although the planets in mutual reception may be viewed as the final dispositors.

Elements

Fire inspires with an idea that is communicated by *Air*, made manifest by *Earth* and evaluated by *Water*.

Hemispheres

More planetary emphasis towards the upper hemisphere (South), career and the outer world seem of greater importance. A sense of responsibility and perhaps a public persona are likely, with an objective viewpoint.

It's often thought that when the lower hemisphere (North) is emphasised, the person is of a more private disposition, which may be so, but ambition and achievement are of equal measure. The individual has the ability to mobilise in tight confines, though can be rather self-contained, and fearful of insecurity. There may be an interest in the land and history, though with more subjective views.

Towards the left hemisphere (East), we have someone who can take charge of situations, a leader and often with spontaneous self-expression, but can end up doing things on their own. They can be good at self-mobilisation.

The right hemisphere (West) has good ability to relate to others, with ease of involvement in joint enterprises. They can make good contacts, know the right people, and are usually protective of others. They can be quite persevering, with controlled energy, though the opinion of others can sometimes be taken too much to heart.

High Focus Planet (HFP)

The High Focus Planet is the first point of consideration in the designated shapes, and tends to drive the personality by acting as a spring board to interpretation. How strong or indeed successful that drive may be can be elicited from its astrological strength in terms of dignity or debility. (See under Dignity and Debility) Signs, houses and aspects will of course, modify the description, for good or ill.

The Moon as HFP is often indicative of someone who might elicit wide appeal, and could well be influential in some particular field of endeavour. Its feminine energy could indicate good relations with women.

Mercury as HFP indicates mental acuity, great versatility, and restlessness, with a youthful outlook. There may be difficulty in staying in one arena of endeavour.

Venus as HFP gives success through charm and likeable personality, with ability to make good contacts.

The Sun as HFP reveals someone who strives to balance the Personality, Soul and Spirit within their personal consciousness through their particular field of endeavour. This could result in leadership.

Mars as HFP will often show drive and energy, but could also be involved in combative arenas where the individual is pitted against competitive others, or adversaries. Challenges are often welcome.

Jupiter as HFP is indicative of success in endeavours, far sightedness and restlessness.

Saturn as HFP may show that responsibility could be thrust upon the individual's shoulders, where the choices are often restricted, making the individual work within narrow confines but with perseverance.

Uranus as HFP may show someone original in thinking and behaviour, standing out from the crowd for good or ill. A scientific predisposition may be evident. May have global impact.

Neptune as HFP could reveal an idealistic predisposition, someone working on behalf of others with a social conscience, and possibly a saviour mentality. May have global impact.

Pluto as HFP indicates strength of purpose and possibly a secretive nature. May have global impact.

House Strength

Some houses are said to be more effective for happiness, and success. Angular houses (1/7, 4/10) are designated the strongest for success because they are supposedly more visible in the world. Succedent houses (2/8, 5/11) have strength through stability and longevity. Cadent houses (3/9, 6/12) are changeable and often seen as weak, however, they can gain strength through adaptability.

This is something to be borne in mind but not taken as gospel truth because the many examples of successful people in this book do not always follow this long-held custom.

Midpoints

A planet which occupies the midpoint degree of two other planets is often referred to as being on that midpoint or falls on that midpoint. If a planet also aspects a certain midpoint by semi-square, sesquiquadrate, square or opposition, the terminology remains the same as does the strength of the planetary midpoint.

Planetary Joys

The seven classical or traditional planets are said to rejoice in certain houses, thus giving strength to their position. The benefics – Venus and Jupiter – are in fortunate houses when they are in the 5th and 11 respectively, the Moon and Sun when they are in the houses of the mind – 3rd and 9th – respectively, and the malefics – Mars and Saturn – are in challenging houses, the 6th and 12th respectively.

Planets in Houses

Some astrologers regard planets placed in the first few degrees of a house much stronger than those situated in the middle or towards the end. Indeed, traditionally a planet within 5° of the next house is deemed to already be in the next house. In nativities perhaps the planet latterly described may influence both houses.

Quadruplicities

Cardinal (Aries/Libra, Cancer/Capricorn) – quick to initiate enterprises or impulsive.

Fixed (Taurus/Scorpio, Leo/Aquarius) – determination bringing permanence or rigidity.

Mutable (Gemini/Sagittarius, Virgo/Pisces) – a sense of duality bringing versatility or instability.

Reception

This occurs when two planets are in each other's signs, and can therefore, symbolically speaking, change signs. This is said to strengthen the planets especially if either of them are weakened by detriment as the first example.

1. Moon in Capricorn, Saturn in Cancer. In this example, both planets are initially in detriment, but as they are in mutual reception, this strengthens them.

2. Or mixed reception such as Saturn in Libra, Venus in Aquarius. Saturn is already strong by exaltation, though it is further strengthened by changing into its domicile, and Venus is also strengthened by symbolically returning to the sign it rules.

Singleton

A planet which may appear to carry the weight of the chart by virtue of its apparent isolation, and thrust into prominence.

1. Being the only one appearing in any one hemisphere of the chart: North (bottom half), South (top half), East (left half) or West (right half) cut by the AC/DC line or the MC/IC line.

2. Being the only one in any of the elements or quadruplicities, or type of house (angular, succedent, cadent).

3. Or being somehow divorced from the rest of the chart by being outside the planetary boundary line.

Data Sources

Annie Besant
Astro-Databank quotes that Alan Leo, who knew her personally, rectified the time from a given 5:00 to 5:45 PM. Sabian Symbols No.95 gives 5:20 PM; same time (17:29) in *Sterne und Mensch* IX.Jg (H.5-6) Also, Peter Washington's biography, *Madame Blavatsky's Baboon: A History of the Mystics, Mediums, and Misfits Who Brought Spiritualism to America*, Schocken Books, New York, 1995. (RR: A)

George Blake
Astro-Databank: Edward Spiro, *The Many Sides of George Blake*, 1970, p.33. (RR: AA)

Wernher Von Braun
Astro-Databank: Luc de Marre quotes H. Schwarz in *Neue Weltschaw*, 2/1958, p.7, "Information received from the entourage of Von Braun." (RR: A)

Lord George Gordon Noel Byron
Astro-Databank quotes Notable Nativity No.752, "Family records in British Museum". (RR: AA)

Sir Winston Churchill
Astro-Databank: Sy Scholfield quotes father's letter to his mother-in-law written on the day of Winston's birth. (RR: A)

Agatha Christie
Astro-Databank: AFA quotes her Autumn/1967, confirmed by Charles Harvey, "She wrote that 4:00 AM is the time with the notation 'hearsay,' presumably due to her legal background." (RR: AA)

Noel Coward
Astro-Databank LMR quotes Biography: Leslie, Payne & Marley, *Noel Coward and Friends* reproduces his baby book page printed in his mother's own hand, p.10. (RR: B)

Humphry Davy
Astro-Databank: From brother John Davy's *Memoirs Of The Life Of Sir Humphry Davy Vol. I*, 1839, pg. 2: "He was born on the 17th of December, 1778, at five o'clock in the morning, as is certified in the cover of a large family-Bible, in the handwriting of [Robert Davy] his father." (RR: AA)

Dr John Dee
Author of *The Queen's Conjurer* Benjamin Woolley quotes an authenticated chart done by Elias Ashmole, who acquired Dee's library. The original is in the Ashmole Manuscript collection at the Bodleian Library, ref MS Ashmole 1788, f137. 137r.

Sir Hugh Dowding
Astro-Databank quotes Paul Wright collection, B.C. (RR: AA)

Sir Arthur Conan Doyle
Astro-Databank: Paul Wright and Sy Scholfield. (RR: AA)

Bobby Fischer
Astro-Databank D. Ames quotes F. Brady, *Profile of a Prodigy*, p.2. (RR: B)

Sir David Lloyd George
Astro-Databank: rectified chart

Harrison Ford
Astro-Databank: B.C. in hand from Barbara Frigillana. (RR: AA)

Mata Hari
Astro-Databank, Data Source BC/BR in hand, Ed Steinbrecher. (RR: AA)

Hedy Lamarr
Astro-Databank: Blanca Holmes quotes her in *Wynn* magazine 10/1944. (RR: A)

King Ludwig II
Astro-Databank: Arthur Blackwell quotes the official announcement given in AA 2/1956, 8/25/1845, 00:25 AM LMT.

George Harrison
Astro-Databank quotes *Mercury Hour*, 4/1993, p.1. (RR: A)

George Michael
Astro-Databank: Frank Clifford quotes B.C., with no time. Janey Stubb quotes his office for time. (RR: A)

Ignace Padarewski
Astro-Databank quotes Penfield Collection spec. Old-file has 1:36 AM LMT, Warsaw, Poland. *World Book Encyclopedia* gives Podolia, Ukraine. Alan Leo gives November 6, 1860 in *Modern Astrology* 11/1939 "according to a biography by R. Landau, no style given (OS/NS)." Leo assumes NS, spec of 2:30 AM. Astrologia.Pl quotes 5.00am.

Kim Philby
Astro-Databank quotes Chester Kemp in *Astrology Quarterly* Winter/1979. Starkman rectified to 14.36.40 IST Asc 27Tau29. (RR: C)

Franklin Delano Roosevelt
Astro-Databank: *Sara and Eleanor: The Story of Sara Delano Roosevelt and Her Daughter-in-Law Eleanor Roosevelt* by Jan Pottker, 2005, pg. 59. (RR: AA)

Arnold Schwarzenegger
Astro-Databank: D.C. Doane quotes a colleague from him 1979. (RR: A)

Bibliography

Astrology

Bailey, Alice. *Esoteric Astrology*, Lucis Trust, 1951.

Cornell, H.L. *The Encyclopaedia of Medical Astrology*, Weiser, 1923.

Ebertin, Reinhold. *The Combination of Stellar Influences*, AFA 1940/1972.

Hodgson, Joan. *Astrology: The Sacred Science*, The White Eagle Publishing Trust, 1978.

Jansky, R.C. *Planetary Patterns*, Astro-Analytics Publications 1974.

Jansson, Torgny. *Esoteric Astrology, A Beginner's Guide*, Authorhouse, 2005.

Jones, Marc Edmund. *The Guide to Horoscope Interpretation*, McKay, Philadelphia, 1941 Quest 1974.

Lilly, William. *Christian Astrology*, Regulus, 1647, 1985.

Oken, Alan. *Soul-Centred Astrology*, Bantum Books, 1990.

Weiner, Errol. *Transpersonal Astrology*, Element 1991.

Biography

Annie Besant
Besant, A. *An Autobiography*, H. Altemus 1893, General Books 2009.

George Blake
Blake, George. *No Other Choice*, Jonathan Cape, 1990.

Bourke, Sean. *The Springing of George Blake*, Cassell, 1970.

Boyle, Andrew. *The Climate of Treason*, Hutchinson & Co 1979.

West, R. *The Meaning of Treason*, Virago Press1982.

Wernher Von Braun
Ward, B. *Dr Space. The Life of Wernher Von Braun*, Naval Institute Press, 2005.

Lord George Byron
O'Brien, E. *Byron in Love*, Weidenfeld & Nicholson 2009.

Quennel, P. *Byron, The Years of Fame*, Wm.Collins Sons & Co. Ltd 1974.

Agatha Christie
Burton, Neel. M.D. https://www.psychologytoday.com/gb/blog/hide-and-seek/201203/dissociative-fugue-the-mystery-agatha-christie

Christie, Agatha. *An Autobiography*, Dodds, Mead & Co. 1977.

Curran, John. *Agatha Christie's Secret Notebooks*, Harper Collins 2009.
ITV Perspectives 2013 'The Mystery of Agatha Christie' https://www.youtube.
    com/watch?v=VUmbf2fMF5M
Thompson, Laura. *Agatha Christie: An English Mystery*, Headline 2008.

Winston Churchill
Hickman, Tom. *Churchill's Bodyguard*, Headline, 2005.
Keegan, John. *Churchill's Generals*, Weidenfeld & Nicholson, 1991.
Kershaw, Robert. *Never Surrender*, Hodder 2009.
Wilson, Harold. *A Prime Minister on Prime Ministers*, Weidenfeld & Nicholson 1977.

Noel Coward
Coward, Noel. *Present Indicative; Future Indefinite; Past Conditional*, Heinemann
    1937, Doubleday & Co., 1937.
Coward, Noel. *The Letters of Noel Coward*. Edited by Barry Day, Methuen, 2007

Humphrey Davy
Treneer, A. *The Mercurial Chemist*, Methuen & Co Ltd 1963.

Dr John Dee
Woolley, B. *The Queen's Conjurer, The Science and Magic of Dr Dee*, Harper
    Collins, 2001.
www.ancient-origins.net/john-dee

Sir Arthur Conan Doyle
Cook, Ivan. *The Return of Sir Arthur Conan Doyle*, White Eagle Publishing Trust,
    1980.
Doyle, Arthur. *Memories and Adventures: An Autobiography'*, Wordsworth
    Edition 2007.
Johnson, R. & Upton, J. *The Sherlock Holmes Miscellany*, The History Press 2012.

Sir Hugh Dowding
Dowding, Hugh, Lord Air Chief Marshall. *Many Mansions*, White Crow
    Productions Ltd 1943.
Orange, Vincent. *Dowding of Fighter Command*, Grub Street Publishing 2008.

Bobby Fisher
Brady, Frank. *Endgame: The Spectacular Rise and Fall of Bobby Fischer*, Constable
    & Robinson, Ltd 2011.
Ponterotto, J. 'A Psychological Autopsy of Bobby Fischer' https://psmag.com

Harrison Ford
Jenkins, G. *Harrison Ford: Imperfect Hero*, Simon & Schuster Ltd 1998.

David Lloyd George
Edwards, Huw. 'David Lloyd George: The People's Champion', *BBC 4*, Feb 2009.
Hague, Ffion. *The Pain and the Privilege*, Harper Perennial 2008.
Toye, Richard. *Lloyd George and Churchill: Rivals for Greatness*, Pan Macmillan, 2007.

Mata Hari
Shipman, Pat. *Femme Fatale: Love, Lies And The Unknown Life Of Mata Hari*, Weidenfeld 2007.

George Harrison
Boyd, Patty and Junor Penny. *Wonderful Today*, Penguin, 2008.
Harrison, G., Taylor, D. (Ed.), Harrison, O. *I, Me, Mine*, Phoenix, 1980/2002.
Thomson, Graeme. *George Harrison, Behind the Locked Door*, Overlook Books, 2015.

Hedy Lamarr
Rhodes, Richard. *Hedy's Folly*, Doubleday 2011.
Lamarr, Hedy., Guild, Leo and Rice, Cy. *Ectasy and Me*, Ishi Press 1966, Fawcett Crest Books 1967.

King Ludwig II of Bavaria
Cooper-Hewitt, D. *Designs for the Dream King*, Debrett's Peerage Ltd., 1978.
Mayr-Ofen, Ferdinand. *Ludwig II of Bavaria*, Cobden Sanderson, 1937.
Schad, Martha. *Ludwig II*, dtv Verlagsgesselschaft, 2000.

George Michael
Jovanovic, R. *George Michael, The Biography*, Piatkus, 2008.
Michael, George. *Michael: In His Own Words*, with editors Nigel Goodall and Chris Charlesworth, 1999.

Ignace Padarewski
Zamoyski, Adam. *Paderewski*, Harper Collins, 1982.

Kim Philby
Boyle, A. *The Climate of Treason*, Hutchinson 1979.
Brown, A.C. *Treason in the Blood*, Houghton Mifflin Company, 1994.
Macintyre, Ben. *A Spy Among Friends*, Bloomsbury, 2015 .

Philby, H.A.R. *My Silent War: The Autobiography of a Spy*, MacGibbon & Kee Ltd., 1968.
West, R. *The Meaning of Treason*, Virago Press 1982.

Franklin Delano Roosevelt
Roosevelt, Eleanor. *Autobiography*, Harper & Bros 1961, Da Capo Press 1992.
Rowley, H. *Franklin and Eleanor: An Extraordinary Marriage*, Picador, 2010.

Arnold Schwarzenegger
Schwarzenegger, Arnold. *Total Recall*, with Peter Petre, Simon & Schuster, 2012.

Wanda Sellar is a past president of the Astrological Lodge of London, for whom she now co-ordinates the weekly lecture programme. She has edited the *Astrology & Medicine* newsletter for the Astrological Association for 22 years and is the author of three books on astrology (*The Consultation Chart, An Introduction to Medical Astrology* and *Introduction to Decumbiture*), as well as two books on aromatherapy (*The Directory of Essential Oils* and *Frankincense & Myrrh Through the Ages*). She has taught astrology in Europe and Japan.

Wanda can be contacted on wandaelizabethsellar@gmail.com

Other Titles from The Wessex Astrologer
www.wessexastrologer.com

Martin Davis
Astrolocality Astrology: A Guide to What it is and How to Use it
From Here to There: An Astrologer's Guide to Astromapping

Wanda Sellar
The Consultation Chart
An Introduction to Medical Astrology
An Introduction to Decumbiture

Geoffrey Cornelius
The Moment of Astrology

Darrelyn Gunzburg
Life After Grief: An Astrological Guide to Dealing with Grief
AstroGraphology: The Hidden Link between your Horoscope and your Handwriting
Grief: A Dark, Sacred Time

Paul F. Newman
Declination: The Steps of the Sun
Luna: The Book of the Moon

Deborah Houlding
The Houses: Temples of the Sky

Dorian Geiseler Greenbaum
Temperament: Astrology's Forgotten Key

Howard Sasportas
The Gods of Change

Patricia L. Walsh
Understanding Karmic Complexes

M. Kelly Hunter
Living Lilith: the Four Dimensions of the Cosmic Feminine

Barbara Dunn
Horary Astrology Re-Examined

Deva Green
Evolutionary Astrology

Jeff Green
Pluto Volume 1: The Evolutionary Journey of the Soul
Pluto Volume 2: The Evolutionary Journey of the Soul Through Relationships
Essays on Evolutionary Astrology (ed. by Deva Green)

Dolores Ashcroft-Nowicki and Stephanie V. Norris
The Door Unlocked: An Astrological Insight into Initiation

Greg Bogart
Astrology and Meditation: The Fearless Contemplation of Change

Henry Seltzer
The Tenth Planet: Revelations from the Astrological Eris

Ray Grasse
Under a Sacred Sky: Essays on the Practice and Philosophy of Astrology

CPSIA information can be obtained
at www.ICGtesting.com
Printed in the USA
LVHW080205190320
650546LV00006B/438

9 781910 531389